Baby Brain

Was my womb controlling my brain?

Jennifer Palfreeman

This book is dedicated to my mum and dad.

They have been there every step of the way.

I love you both so much x

Baby Brain

ACKNOWLEDGEMENTS

Firstly, I would like to thank my wonderful editor Netti Cairns. She has helped transform my story from rambling emotional memoirs into a book I am extremely proud to have produced. Her professionalism, friendship and support have been welcomed throughout the editing process, and I will be forever grateful.

Secondly, my auntie Catherine Burnett for creating the beautiful cover for my book, which is better than I could ever have imagined. She is such a talented artist.

Thirdly, my thanks go to the professionals who have helped me to gather records and information from my medical history. Without the background research and information received from the staff at Leeds General Infirmary maternity department, my confidence in writing this book would have been thwarted.

Last but by no means least, I want to thank my family and friends who have supported me on my journey to complete this book. It has been an emotional roller-coaster, that is for sure. Ryan, Kian and Zac: without you and your love this book would never have been written. You are my happy ending.

Baby Brain

Contents

Part 1

Part 2

My journey back to you

Preface

I have written my story several times in my head during long nights of little sleep; my mind racing with a compulsion to empty my head of the whirling memories and flashbacks. It now feels like the right time for me to put pen to paper. It is the eve of a new year and my resolution is not only to complete my degree this year but also to write my story. I now feel strong enough to share the tragedy and trauma I went through to become a mum, and the heart-breaking decisions I had to make along the way. As my story unfolds, it will become clear why I have named this book Baby Brain and I very much hope that it will resonate with anyone who may have been or be going through similar experiences, raise awareness to those who know little about this subject, and also perhaps give others who are considering it the confidence to share their stories, too.

For the past two years, I have been working to finish my degree in 'Working with Young People, Families and Society'. The realisation that reaching back into education and writing essays following a fifteen-year break would be more than a small challenge hit me hard. However, studying has been hugely beneficial to me in my professional life; working with families and children suffering adversity within society. In embracing the theories and concepts, I have also related much of the learning back to my own personal trauma, which has in turn helped prepare me to write this book.

. . . .

One day, whilst on my way home from a long day studying, on went my headphones and I chose a TED talk to watch on YouTube. I love to listen to the inspirational speakers and their words of wisdom. I'd listened to Justine Musk before and having found her previous talks compelling, chose one of her recent talks. Justine was married to the highly successful businessman Elon Musk. The talk I chose was called "Wounded People Tell Better Stories". Listening to her talk was an emotional experience for me; her words echoed the way I felt about telling my story. She talked about passion and compassion and the origin of the words meaning 'to suffer' and explained that you can have passion for something that hurts. Then about 'mastery' and the need to get down to the bare bones of something to master and learn from it. I had the passion to tell my story but always thought I would only be able to tell it when it no longer hurt. From that moment, I have had a compulsion to relive my trauma and tell my story.

Journalist Malcom Gladwell wrote a book claiming it takes 10,000 hours to truly master a skill, and the build-up to me writing this this book has exceeded that. My preparation hasn't put bread and butter on the table but has eventually given me the skills and tools to share my story; from a dark and wounded place.

Justine Musk tragically lost her first baby boy, Nevada, at 10 weeks old to SIDS (Sudden Infant Death Syndrome). She has risen from a place of darkness. Her advice is to tell your story: to set it alight like a communal fire and let it burn and spread.

"Watch the sparks reach up to the sky and reach the stars.

We are stars and stars are our stories."

. . . .

I have since been on a long journey back to the beginning: a journey I knew I must face.

Before I began writing, I contacted the LGI hospital PALS team (Patient Advice and Liaison Service) for help. PALS is a service provided by the NHS and their representatives to work on behalf of patients who wish to make a complaint or gain access medical records. The notes have brought clarity to my often hazy and distant memories and I have included some of the letters from my doctor and hospital consultants in my writing.

Part 1

Chapter 1: My story

I was born in Leeds in 1981 to parents Annette and Phil Elliott. My mum and dad met whilst mum was on a teaching practice placement in Farsley, Leeds. Dad was staying in the village with his sister at the time and they met at what has now become one of our local pubs. Mum was aged twenty two and Dad was nearly ten years older at thirty one.

My dad had lived a good life as a single man. He was a teacher and ran a youth club. He loved tennis and organised a staff Wimbledon-style tournament at his school every year as well as playing football and rugby. He enjoyed the social aspects that came with sport and probably drank more than he should but balanced this out with his sporty life and holding down his full-time teaching job.

Mum was brought up in Huddersfield in a traditional family by strict Catholic parents. My grandma had lived in a children's home for most of her life and when she met my granddad at the age of nineteen, they quickly fell in love and got married. They had five children, my mum being in the middle of two brothers and two sisters. My grandma and grandad expected high behavioural standards and with little money and living in a small rented house, they thrived on routine. My mum was quiet at school and had to work hard to achieve academically, however in her late teens, she moved from Huddersfield to study teaching at Ilkley College. This was a relatively short distance in miles, but for my mum, it was a million miles away from her hometown! Mum thrived in this environment and enjoyed the freedom and camaraderie of living with her friends away from home.

My mum signalled a fresh start and security for my dad. He grasped that ideal with open arms and they were married within just over a year of their first date. I was born twelve months later. With my dad being almost ten years older than my mum and had turned thirty-two when I was born, mum was just twenty-three. I was their first of three girls. My parents are both qualified teachers and have devoted many years to the profession. However, my mum left work when I was born and became a stay-at-home mum; only going back to teaching when my youngest sister started primary school. They initially bought a house in Stanningley which is close to the village of Farsley and when I was six months old, they bought the house in Farsley that they still live in today.

When we were growing up, my mum loved being a housewife and mum to us girls. She was very hands-on and enjoyed getting on her hands and knees and playing games with us. Whenever the weather allowed, we would be outside. Our school parties were epic and are still remembered by many of my friends now. My mum would invite the whole class of thirty or so children to our modest three-bed semi for a tea party and arrange traditional games. I suppose because she and my dad were teachers, they were used to dealing with lots of children! They loved it but I think most people thought they were crazy! My mum was the practical one and was very traditional. She took us to school, made our tea and would tell my dad off for letting us climb in the boot of the car with no seat belts or swing too high on the swings in the park.

My dad and I have always had a close relationship. On the surface, my dad will fill time with talk of sport - usually football. He is a talker and he has covered up his worries and insecurities in life by talking about anything but his feelings. Dad had an unusual childhood with a mother and father that had a large age gap between them. My grandad was fifty when my dad was born and my grandma was in her early forties. Grandad was from a military background and was quite elusive at times. My suspicious mind often wonders if he led a double life at that time. He didn't marry my grandma because as it turned out, he was still married to his first wife and had two much older sons already. It was incredibly sad for my dad when my grandma suddenly died of an aneurism when he was just fifteen years old. It was also very hard for my grandad as he then had to bring up his children by himself.

When they were older teenagers, my dad's brother, David, had a car accident whilst driving some friends to an employment conference. Luckily David survived but tragically his friends all died in the crash. David mustn't have been able to cope with the aftermath of the accident as he committed suicide a couple of years later. This was very traumatic for my dad but as is often the case with trauma, my dad (unfortunately like many young men suffering with mental health problems) turned to drink in order to try to block everything out.

My dad was never strict and my mum probably curses the fact that we remember a lot of the fun stuff happening with dad. I know now that my mum was probably exhausted from days of walking us up to school (which was over a mile away) then walking back and picking us back up later, not to mention looking after the house. You would think that with my dad being so sporty, he would have been disappointed to have three girls but he embraced it. We all loved sport and were very much outdoor girls. My dad took us to the park most summer nights or played sport with us in the garden. We would find money he'd mysteriously 'hidden' in the grass and then stop at the corner shop for 20p mixes of sweets. His drinking was never that out of control but he drank most nights and would often slope of to the pub. In my view, his drinking didn't affect us girls or our childhood. My mum might say different though, as she was not a drinker and tried hard to keep my dad on the straight and narrow. My dad adores my mum and would do anything for her, so it did work to an extent. My mum and dad are home birds and although they like going on holiday, they tend to stay on British soil and I've never known them go away for more than a week.

When Dad was too old to play sport, he refereed football every week and at any other opportunity he could get. At seventy-two, he is still an active person and continues to work as an exam invigilator at Leeds University. I can imagine that my dad has used sport and exercise as therapy over the years. He has not had a drink for nearly fifteen years now and takes medication for anxiety and depression.

My mum and dad still live in the same house they bought when I was six months old and it is the still the hub for all our families. We were lucky to be brought up in a loving household and their house will always be special to me. It's probably due to my mum that we all are here to tell the tale though… because without my mum… my dad would be lost.

One of my first memories of growing up was playing 'babies'. I had two younger sisters, Susie and Gemma. Susie is just eighteen months younger than me. Gemma is five years younger. I loved playing at being a mum and one of my favourite games was putting a jumper or cushion up my top or dress and pretending to be pregnant. I was probably around six or seven years old at the time. Gemma didn't feature heavily in the games of mums and babies. This was maybe because she wasn't as compliant as my baby dolls were! I do remember carrying her around one morning, though. She pulled my hair and I turned so quickly that I cricked my neck and couldn't move it. Having to go to hospital and wear a neck brace for a week felt brilliant, as I was a bit of a drama queen and loved the attention! My sisters and I spent hours playing with my dolls and I felt from a young age that I loved babies and couldn't wait to be a 'real' mum. I had two favourite dolls. One was small and bald and I called her Francesca at first but then I must have gone all 'Kim Kardashian' as I changed it to 'Atlanta'. I had another doll with long brown hair that I bought from Woolworths. I loved her, too. I named her 'Jessie'. We had prams, car seats and an abundance of clothes. Was it normal at the age of seven or eight to already want to be a mum? I'm sure millions of children play the same games. But did their need to be a mum feel as intense as mine?

Around the age of ten, my baby obsession continued and I was now able to look after real babies. My mum had a friend, Jane, who lived close by. Jane had two daughters named Molly and Lauren. Lauren was just a baby and I thought she was the cutest thing ever. I looked after her at every opportunity and loved the way that Jane dressed her in frilly clothes and hats. I remember thinking I couldn't wait to have a baby of my own to dress up and look after. I would push Lauren's pram and think I was so grown up.

I still had other interests around this time, such as sport and running. I loved spending time with my dad, so naturally I was interested in whatever sport he was involved in, whether it was cricket or football. As I progressed through school, though, sport and academia became less of a priority.

I was a good student at primary school, being quite academic and clever in nature. Having been brought up in the Catholic faith and going to a Catholic primary and high school, we had good morals. The social aspect of school was always more important to me than work. I had lots of friends and boyfriends! Life at primary and high school was strict and we were also quite sheltered: especially when it came to sex education.

In my final year of primary school, everyone in the class started having boyfriends. My best friend Terri and I were always gossiping about who to go out with next. Nothing ever happened with these boys, apart from maybe a game of 'Kiss-Catch' in the playground. Kids did talk about sex at primary school but with very little education and no Google, it was always a guessing game.

During the 1980's and early 1990's there was a massive T.V campaign around AIDS and the importance of staying safe from catching the killer virus with no cure. The media focused on homosexual men and needle sharing between drug users. These were the groups that had been identified as being at the most danger. It used to scare me when I saw these adverts, and when I found a condom packet at my mum and dad's house, I felt sure that they were somehow in danger. In reality, they were just using contraception although it felt awkward and it upset me that I didn't feel able to discuss this with my mum. I had never seen a condom until high school and had always imagined them to look like the protective boxes that cricketers put in their trousers to cushion the blow of being hit in the balls! If only I'd known that in a few years' time I would be doing condom demonstrations to groups of kids as a youth worker and would be much more clued up. Having thrived at primary school and enjoyed my time there, I left wearing my pinafore dress which everyone used to say I looked pregnant in. I secretly enjoyed this and imagined wearing a real maternity dress. The prospect of starting high school was exciting and would mean I would be really grown up.

My friend Terri and I have been friends since nursery school and went to primary and high school together. We are still the best of friends. Terri has travelled and lived in several places around the U.K, but we have always stayed in touch and now Terri lives only an hour away from where I live in Leeds. Despite being such great friends, I realised just recently that our lives and experiences have been very different, as I am much more of a home bird than Terri. Having analysed this, I feel now that my choice to stay grounded in the familiarity of home has been due to insecurities because of my life experiences from a young age.

During my early teenage years, a couple of my aunties announced their pregnancies. This made me extremely jealous. My cousins of a similar age to me would have a new baby at home. Why couldn't my mum have another baby? A seed was planted in my head and I started pressurising my mum to have another baby. My mum had gone back to teaching at this point as my youngest sister, Gemma, had started primary school. I'm sure that my mum was loving her newfound freedom and the extra money that came with it. I imagine that the last thing she wanted to do was to start again with a new baby and looking back, I have a feeling that I was extremely persistent and probably very annoying in my quest for another sibling. However, at the age of thirteen when rumours started going around school about how a baby was made, it was a time of conflict in my mind when I thought about my mum and dad participating in this to make a baby! My persuasion techniques must have been extreme because I remember my mum saying that they were thinking about having another baby. Soon after, they had a night away. When they came back, they told me that they had such a good time, they'd decided that their family was already complete. It made sense for them but I was gutted.

Chapter 2: Period

At the age of 14, I started to realise that if there was going to be a baby in the house, then it was going to have to be me that got pregnant. I aspired to be a lawyer at school and when I was in year nine, I did my work experience in a solicitor's office. I got in trouble for wearing provocative clothing and distracting the criminals and the solicitors! Was this the start of an insecurity that would create an imposter type feeling I have felt for much of my adult life? I was already being pushed to try hard at school and do well so that I could have a successful career. I was clever enough to achieve this but unfortunately the pull of being a mum was far stronger. My maternal instinct was already beginning to shape my future with its insistent, intrusive and impulsive way of eating into the core of my being.

The band 'Take That' and becoming a woman are closely linked. My dad had kindly bought me and my sister Susie 'Take That' gig tickets for the Sheffield Arena. We had never been to a concert before and we were ecstatic! I was fourteen and my sister thirteen. My mum was not happy because my dad had only bought two tickets and expected Susie and I to make our own way to Sheffield to see our idols. We were so incredibly excited that we would have walked to Sheffield Arena from our house in Leeds to see Mark Owen in the flesh! However, mum talked dad into getting himself a ticket and he was secretly quite excited to see Lulu, who was due to make a guest appearance when they performed the song 'Relight my Fire'. The excitement had been building all day at school and I kept feeling sick with stomach-ache. I told my mum how I was feeling before we set off and she reassured me that it was probably just nerves for the concert.

The show started and I felt a rush of excitement through my body. I also felt a gush in my knickers! What was happening? I took myself off to the toilet to find that my period had started. As I realised what had happened, I had mixed feelings. "Shit! I'm missing Take That!" was the main one! I went back out to the concert but I couldn't enjoy it and all that was on my mind was that I was a woman now and could have a baby. When I got home, I told my mum. (I hadn't wanted to disclose the information to my dad in front of crowds of people). My mum let me sleep in her bed, made me a hot water bottle and gave me some sanitary pads. I had no idea that starting my period that night would begin twenty years of the pain and hell of having a functioning womb. I told Terri in confidence the next day but somehow private information of this magnitude doesn't stay secret for long at school. I quite quickly had random kids singing 'Take That' songs at me whilst laughing. Certainly, that night everything had changed. Thank God the band hadn't released 'The Flood' by then!

Chapter 3 : Reece

During my first couple of years at high school I was compliant, tried hard with homework and was a good student. I had a few boyfriends, though none of them were serious and anything physical just involved kissing and a bit of a fumble. I thought I was in love at times and cried while listening to Maria Carey in my bedroom on several occasions when relationships I thought were serious, were in fact over. On Saturday nights, I would regularly baby-sit for a family who lived over the road from us. From around the age of thirteen, I would invite my boyfriend at the time to babysit with me.

Kerry was the baby of the three children I looked after. She was such a cute little girl and being with her made me want a baby of my own. When I had a boyfriend babysitting with me, I imagined us being a family with our own child. There was one problem though: I was quite scared of having sex. I knew that was ultimately how to make a baby unfortunately, and this was going to have to happen soon.

I was dumped by a boy who I thought was perfect. He spread it round school that I was frigid; which was mortifying at the time. Also around that time, my friendship group changed. Terri had a stable boyfriend who was a bit older and she spent all of her time with him. I started hanging around with the 'cool' group. They met in Rawdon park on Friday nights and (if anyone managed to get served at the local shops) would hang around drinking cider and smoking cigarettes. I had always been a bit of a plain 'Jane' with mousy-brown hair and a flat chest and used to get upset when boys said that I looked like an ironing board. It didn't help me that Terri had massive boobs and gorgeous long blonde hair. My legs were long, though and I eventually had my hair highlighted and started wearing makeup. Constance Carol pressed powder and Heather Shimmer Rimmel lipstick with Nude Number One lip liner from Bodyshop was a must. Contouring was unheard of then and me and my friends always looked a dodgy orange colour with a tide mark around the bottom of our jaws! I did however look older than most of the teenagers in my new group of friends and was the one who usually got sent to buy alcohol, and because I was often successful, then I started to get noticed more by the lads. I began smoking Embassy cigarettes because that's what girls smoked. Boys smoked Regal - that was the rule. We had a laugh and it was a happy time for me. I made lots of new friends, felt like I was popular and enjoyed the attention from the boys.

Some of the lads from the group were friends with a group of teens from Horsforth School who hung around in Horsforth Park. So, on a few occasions we caught the bus down there from Rawdon. One night, with the confidence of the cider, I ended up kissing a lad called Reece. He had Eclipse jeans and a Teddy Smith jacket. He had been to primary school with some of the lads I knew and something instantly drew me to him. He wasn't the best-looking boy but had an enduring, shy personality and a cute smile. When I met Reece as an excited young girl of fifteen with all the opportunities in the world ahead of me, I didn't anticipate that what would happen over the next five years or so would shape my future forever.

Reece lived in a semi-detached house in Horsforth with his mum Lynn, her husband David and his older brother, Jed. His dad, Brian lived in an upper-class part of Leeds with his partner Christine. He had left Reece's mum when he and his brother were little boys. Reece's mum was a teacher and his dad the headmaster at a school for children with additional needs. My dad worked at the same school as Christine and as my mum and dad were both teachers too, Reece and I seemed to have a similar background and I felt a good connection with him from the start.

My school was 20 minutes away from where Reece lived and each Wednesday, I would get off the bus early to meet him. He would usually be hanging around with his friends at the top of the ginnel near his house. I would be so nervous and instantly got butterflies whenever I saw him. I'd see Reece on a Wednesday and then at the weekend. This was a time before any of us had mobile phones and the only phone that you had outside of the house was a car phone. (My dad had a car phone and I'd drive him mad as I used to ring him constantly asking him to give me a lift!) Back then, if you told your friend you would meet them at a certain place, you had to be there!

Friday night was a big occasion for us all. We would plan what to wear, what to drink and where to stay, or rather where to tell our parents we were staying! We would go to the park and drink and smoke. Some of the gang would smoke weed and looking back, it makes me laugh when I think about some of the lads putting Speed in a rizla before swallowing it, then walk around the park with a Walkman on saying they were 'buzzing'.

After a couple of weeks of this new routine, we ended up staying at a schoolfriend's house. Joanne was going out with one of Reece's friends and she must have had a 'free house', so we ended up there. That was the night I lost my virginity to Reece. I was fifteen and all I could think about was whether I was pregnant! I had a secret feeling of excitement. We hadn't used any form of contraception and neither of us had mentioned it. That night holds happy memories, as Reece was really kind to me. Sex wasn't as scary as thought it would be.

A close friend of mine who had sex a few times without protection had unprotected sex that night too. She told me that we needed to go to the sexual health clinic. This was all very dramatic! We got the bus to Otley, a village around half an hours' bus journey away. We waited nervously and I remember speaking to a kind professional who reassured me that she had worked out my cycle days and that I was probably too far on in the month to conceive. I was very confused though, as she asked if I wanted to start taking the Pill or take the morning-after pill, just to be safe. I said 'yes' to the contraceptive pill and 'no' to the morning after pill. I have never to this day taken a morning after pill; although I probably should have taken it in some of the situations I've found myself in. I left the hospital with three months' supply of the contraceptive pill and an abundance of leaflets about how to prevent pregnancy. As we didn't have such a thing as Google in those days, those contraception leaflets would come very handy but not in the way they were intended to help. Really in just exactly the opposite way.

I think my mum and dad must have realised that Reece and I had got closer and were having a physical relationship; however, I kept the fact that I was taking the Pill secret from them for some time. I think I only took it for a short period of time anyway and I know I regularly missed taking them. I just wanted to be like all of my friends who had been taking the Pill for ages. It made me feel grown up. My schoolwork and other interests now went out of the window. I just wanted to be with Reece. I wanted us to be in a grown-up relationship and I wanted a baby. Missing school was a common occurrence and as a result, my school work and GCSE revision suffered. My parents were strict but I was careful. I would pretend to get the bus to school but instead go to Horsforth. There was a group of us who skived off school together and would just hang about. As I said before, I went to a Catholic school. Sex education and contraception is forbidden in the Catholic faith, so we never got any information about sex from school and as a result, I didn't know much about sex.

I was quite naive in what I thought I knew about getting pregnant. I started missing just one pill each month and then panicked and stressed at the prospect of being pregnant until my period started. I think unless you have actively tried to get pregnant, you don't realise what a scientific process it is. I can fully understand that accidents happen and that women do fall pregnant whilst on contraception without even trying, and I've heard stories about babies being born holding their mother's contraceptive coil. However, with my limited knowledge, I believed that if you had sex at any point during the month, you could easily fall pregnant.

Alas, Reece and I were now 16 years old and both living with our parents. When we were together, we would be with friends, so this created little opportunity to do the 'deed'. Each month would go by and I would be increasingly lax over my pill taking. This is when the leaflets from the sexual health clinic came in handy. They gave advice on how not to get pregnant and explained the myths around what was considered to be 'safe sex'. It was information such as: 'If you stand up in the shower after sex you can still get pregnant' or 'If you're on your period you can still get pregnant'. It made it sound so easy! I had one leaflet which was full of information on different methods of contraception including the 'rhythm' method. This is method of contraception that requires you to avoid sex during your fertile times. "When was this?", I asked myself. The leaflet stated that if you avoided sex in the middle of your cycle then you were less likely to get pregnant. "Well then, let's do the opposite!", I thought.

Around this time, I got my GCSE results from school. They were not great… in fact, they were crap! Even though I knew they would be, I was disappointed in myself because I knew I could have worked harder but it was too little too late. I had not tried my best and I could have achieved so much more. My mum comforted me and told me that I could still stay on at six form but my heart wasn't in it.

Each month, I thought about getting pregnant but gynaecological issues had already begun to affect me. My periods were very irregular and when they did arrive, they were extremely heavy and painful. This only seemed to start when I came off the contraceptive pill completely. It was frustrating and I worried there was something wrong with me. I did wonder if I was pregnant sometimes when my period was late but when I looked up signs and symptoms of early pregnancy in my mum's big medical journal, I didn't have any pregnancy symptoms, and I didn't ever dare to do a pregnancy test. My period would eventually show up and I would feel bereft.

When I was sixteen, I really hurt Reece. I cheated on him with one of his friends and even now I feel guilty about doing this. Steven was seventeen and always flirted with me. He was a charmer and charmed me into breaking into another friend's caravan (which was parked on their parent's drive…I'm mortified looking back!) to have sex after drinking a litre of cider one Friday night. I totally regretted doing this and Steven was very much a disappointment. The romantic setting of a caravan just didn't do it for me!

I had begun sixth form at St Marys' school and was studying for an intermediate level GNVQ in Business and Finance. This was the only course they would accept me on, due to my GCSE results. I hated it. All of my friends had started their 'A' levels and I felt disappointed in myself as I knew that I could have achieved so much more and been with them.

Reece had stayed on at Horsforth School and he really hadn't done much better than me in his GCSE's. He had managed to get on to the advanced GNVQ level course. I don't know how it came about exactly but either my mum or I got in touch with Horsforth School, and they agreed to accept me on the advanced course with Reece. I had missed a few weeks but soon caught up. The class was all boys, apart from me. There were around twelve of us in the class altogether and from the start, I knew I was going to enjoy Horsforth School. My plan was to show how capable I was and I enjoyed the praise I received for my high standard of work. With everything that had gone on with Steven and the night in the caravan, Reece and he had completely fallen out and lots of Reece's friends had told him not to take me back. I begged for forgiveness and Reece and I distanced ourselves from that friendship group and spent a lot of time with other friends from our course and sixth form. Reece finally forgave me and we soon got back on track.

Things seemed to have settled with my periods and they had started to become a bit more regular. Reece and I were spending more time together and so I was able to plan the sex timings a bit better. I had also read somewhere, probably in a magazine, that if you put your legs up in the air after sex, you would have a better chance of falling pregnant. It made sense as everything would be going in the right direction! So, there I was in my school uniform in my boyfriend's bedroom with my legs in the air. This is a guilty memory when I look back, as Reece knew nothing about this and thought I was still taking the Pill. My feelings of wanting a baby were so strong and even though I knew I had other options in my life, such as going university and getting a good job, I just couldn't control my desire to be mum.

School was going well and we had an upcoming exchange trip to Sweden booked in a couple of months. It was the first time I would be going abroad and I felt nervous but excited. There were only four of us going on the trip: me, Reece and two lads. We were all good friends. We each had a family to stay with in Stockholm for two weeks and the exchange students were due to travel back to England and stay with us in six months' time. We were planning to do work experience with local businesses and visit the local sights. It was all very exciting.

My periods were now quite regular. One Saturday when Reece and I were babysitting, I mentioned to him that I had not yet come on my period. Reece reassured me. He was sure I would be fine given that I was taking the Pill. I knew he really loved me, despite what I had put him through, and I talked to him to try to get a feel of how he would react if I was pregnant.

On the Monday morning I went over the road to see Adele. She was the mum of the children I babysat for and I really admired her. Adele and her husband, Mick, had a baby when they were young and then went on to get married. They now lived in a lovely house and had three gorgeous children. She was someone I very much aspired to be like. I loved the idea of my husband going out to work while I stayed at home and looked after my babies.

As I walked over to her house with these thoughts in my mind, a little voice in my head said to me "Hang on a minute! "The truth was: I went to a good school, I had positive role models and plenty of opportunities. I didn't live in a deprived area or follow unsavoury learned behaviour from my parents. Why was I thinking like this? Surely, I should and could aspire to be more?

I told Adele that I thought I was pregnant. She popped down to our local chemist and got me a pregnancy test. This would be the first of many tests that I would take over the coming years. After what seemed like hours, Adele looked at the test and told me it was negative. I pretended to be relieved but I was so disappointed - I really thought that this was it. Adele told my mum that she had done the test with me and I think my mum was pretty upset that I hadn't gone to her. I remember her saying I needed to be more careful and remember to take the Pill correctly. But of course, that was the last thing on my mind.

Chapter 4: Sweden

Another month had gone by and a lot of my time had been taken up getting ready for Sweden. My first trip abroad was going to be a daunting time because I was going with my boyfriend and not my family, or an adult. I had just turned seventeen and felt very grown up. My mum packed my case with me. She made a point of packing sanitary pads and saying that I would be needing these, as I was due on my period any time soon. I remember hoping that I wouldn't need them and something was niggling at me that I was pregnant this month. However, I had tricked myself into feeling the same just the month before and I felt scared that I was now going to a foreign country and could be pregnant. Reece and I had sex at the right time according to the rhythm method leaflet, so it was very possible. As I got on the smallest plane in the world at Leeds Bradford Airport, I wondered if it was safe to fly whilst pregnant and whether I should just get off the plane and run to my mum and dad, who were frantically waving me off from the departure lounge.

Sweden started with a bit of a disaster. I arrived at my host family's house to find that I was given a bed in their cold and dark attic. Thinking back, I was just emotional and scared but I really didn't want to stay in the house. I felt the family were cold toward me and the language barrier was a major issue. I was probably being a brat but I refused to stay there somehow left to go to Reece's host family. Reece was staying with a single mum and her daughter. They were both warm and welcomed me into their home. I knew straight away that I would be happier there and refused to go back to my host family's house.

Despite the fact that we weren't really supposed to at our age, we often stayed at each other's houses and our parents turned a blind eye, most of the time. Unless of course we were at Reece's dad's house, which was a rarity. Brian was quite strict and Reece acted like a totally different boy around him.

Of course, this change to the agreed plan caused problems! The exchange school in Sweden contacted our school back home and our teachers contacted us directly. They were clearly upset by our behaviour and felt that it was inappropriate that we were staying in the same house. Anyway, I dug my hormonal heals in and stayed at Reece's host family's house. Little did they know that their concern was probably too little too late anyway!

For the whole time that we were in Sweden, I had several symptoms of pregnancy and even considered buying a test. I didn't bother in the end though, as I thought that I wouldn't understand the results in Swedish and I also felt pretty scared. Every morning, I felt sick and couldn't even face chewing gum. By the afternoon, I was starving and would eat loads of McDonalds food and then go out in the evening for a meal or eat at one of the hosts' houses. I wanted to eat all the time and felt bloated and sick. Reece and I were watching the Eurovision song contest one night, which was televised from Sweden that year and had Ulrica Johnson presenting. We had been cuddling up and I said to Reece: "What if I'm pregnant?" I always remember he said he would be glad if we heard the pitter patter of tiny feet. I was so hoping that this was the month! It was just the obstacle of telling our parents that concerned me, and in particular, how Reece's dad would react.

For the rest of the time in Sweden I tried to carry on as normal. I didn't go on any rides at the theme park, I drank alcohol but tried to stick to lager and didn't drink much – just enough not to arouse suspicion or seem to the others like I was being boring. We went to see Janet Jackson one night at Stockholm Arena. It was Janet's birthday. We got there early and everyone we went with wanted to stand. I was being pushed around a little more than was comfortable at times and knew it could be dangerous for the baby if I was pregnant and got knocked, so I spent most of the night worrying. It was still an amazing night and I will remember that concert forever. When I touched down at Leeds Bradford Airport and my sanitary pads were still firmly packed inside my suitcase, I knew I would have to face the music.

Chapter 5: Andrew

My mum asked the obligatory questions regarding our trip, although I could tell she was dying to ask if I had started my period whilst in Sweden. When she finally plucked up the courage to ask me, my reply was a very sheepish, "no". We chatted about it and convinced each other that it was probably the excitement of travelling, the time difference and the jet lag that had delayed my period. (I'd been to Sweden and not China, Mother!) Mum did say that I should probably go to see our doctor though because I had been having irregular and heavy periods for a while now (little did my mum know that this was due to my irregular pill taking!). In the meantime, when no one was around at home, I consulted the big medical journal from the bookshelf and read and read again the symptoms of early pregnancy. Did I have white discharge? Yes, I had that. I kept thinking I was bleeding in Sweden but when I went to the toilet, I found thick white discharge. Feeling sick? Yes, that was a definite. Feeling tired? Well, I was a teenager and felt like I needed to sleep most of the time, but yes,

I was more tired. Sore boobs? Tick. Basically, every symptom I had indicated pregnancy.

My mum and I sat in the doctor's surgery a few days later and explained the circumstances; the irregularity of my periods and that I hadn't had a period since before I went away on the school trip to Sweden. Doctor Meads, who had been my doctor since childhood, had a poor reputation when it came to his bedside manner. Surprisingly, he was pleasant and reassuring and said he would send away a urine sample to rule out pregnancy and would take it from there. I don't remember how the follow up appointment came about but I do remember insisting that I walk around to see the doctor by myself. It wasn't as much a shock for me as it seemed to be for him when he said the test was positive! It clearly wasn't a moment for congratulations in his mind, but Doctor Meads was supportive enough and said that he would book me in to see a midwife. Everything went a bit fuzzy in my ears at this point and I wasn't listening anymore: I was just trying to take in that I was pregnant and was going to be a mum. Now to tell Reece, and our families.

If there was one person who was going to turn up to walk me home, it would be my dad, and sure enough, there he was. As we walked home that warm and sunny evening, my dad chatted away to me about Aston Villa - the team he has always supported - even though he has always had a soft spot for my team, Leeds Utd. He filled my silence and it felt good just to have him there by my side, despite the fact that I could not take in a word he was saying. I burst into tears when I saw my mum. The emotions came flooding out. I think the fact Reece and I had been together for nearly two years proved to my family that we were serious about each other and my mum knew that I was very mature for my age in some respects. I believe my mum had been expecting this news. I had a cousin who had a baby at seventeen and my auntie (mum's sister) had her children young, so this was not as big a deal for her as it could have been for some mothers; despite her Catholic upbringing. I was hugely relieved at her support and positivity around the news.

Reece cried as well. He was so worried about telling his dad. Brian had been brought up by a working-class mother in Glasgow and he had worked extremely hard to become a headmaster. He expected great things of Reece and wanted him to go to university after sixth form. Reece's mum was quite soft with him, though, and Reece would sometimes take advantage of this. His dads' partner Christine didn't have children and I discovered later that she would have loved a child of her own, but I am not sure Reece's dad wanted any more. I think she was upset by, and possibly jealous of this news. I am not sure Brian realised that while he was living with his new wife in a posh part of Leeds, Reece was often out drinking and smoking in Horsforth. He was angry when Reece told him our news and looking back, I can now see why. He thought that the best solution to my pregnancy was for me to have an abortion. He later shouted at me when we spoke on the phone and although it was just the initial shock, I was really hurt. My mum was supportive towards us and did not like the way his dad tried to manipulate me. My family and I had already decided that abortion was not an option.

Tragically, Brian died several years ago of a heart attack. It was very sudden and must have been devastating for the family. He was a good man and did great things for children with additional needs. He was passionate about his job as a headmaster and some would say that this was his downfall, as his hard work had badly affected his health.

I went back to school as normal and we told our friends and teachers the news. Everyone seemed happy for us and was supportive. One member of staff had gone into teaching later in life after having two children during her teenage years. I got on with her well and we chatted more like friends than student and teacher. I wasn't feeling bad physically and was excited for the future. Lots of my mum's friends passed on clothes and baby equipment. I felt so grown up washing and ironing blankets, sheets and tiny clothes. I would soon have a little baby to wrap up in these blankets.

I had my first scan on the 8th of July 1998. I was 15 weeks and 4 days pregnant. This scan was with a consultant, Mr. Brown at the Clarendon Wing at Leeds General Infirmary. I am not sure why I saw a consultant at this stage as so far, all had appeared normal with the pregnancy and there wasn't anything significant to indicate this need in my notes, either. At the appointment, there was initial confusion around my due date, as I wasn't completely sure of the exact date of my last period. In the end, Reece and I were told that our baby was due on Christmas Day. I was so happy we would have a Christmas baby! We all questioned whether it would be a girl or a boy. What would we call the baby? I loved the name 'Chloe' for a girl but my spelling is atrocious and I could never remember how to spell it! Reece liked 'Owen' for a boy, after the footballer Michael Owen.

Consultant						UNITED LEEDS TEACHING HOSPITALS NHS TRUST OBSTETRIC RECORD CLARENDON WING	Hospital Number
1	2	3	4	5	6		
JSS	RRM	KWH	PSV	MRG		M Ø	

First Names JENNIFER   **Surname** ELLIOTT

Next of kin

Relationship mother   **Maiden Name**

Telephone number S/A

M S W Sep Div Unsupported   **Address 1**

Year of Marriage 1   2   **TELEPHONE**

Patient's occupation 6th form Pupil   **Address 2**

Husband's / Partner's occupation 6th form Pupil   **TELEPHONE**   POST CODE

S/E Group 1 2 3 4 5   **Date of first visit** 8.7.98   **Booking Number**

SUMMARY

Pre-pregnancy disorders   Maternal age at delivery

A/N complications

I/P complications   Gestational age at delivery

Delivery   BABY — Sex

Date of Delivery   — Weight

Blood Group   Requires rubella vaccination   YES/NO

D.O.B.   Last contraception used before this pregnancy: —   **L.M.P.** end 03 98   **SURE/UNSURE**

Age at booking 17 yrs   Combined O.C. 1   Cycle

ETHNIC ORIGIN

Place of Birth Leeds   Progesterone only 2   **E.D.D. by calculation**
                I.U.C.D. 3

British Isles B 1   Barrier 4
European (except Britain) E 2   Other 5   E.D.D. by investigation 26 12 98
African Negro A 3   None 6
West Indian Negro W 4   **DATE DISCONTINUED** 26 12 98
African Asian Q 5
Bangladeshi H 6
Indian I 7   6 mths ago
Pakistani P 8   Failed contraception   **GENERAL PRACTITIONER**
Other Caucasian Asian R 9
Mongoloid Asian R 10   Protestant 1
Other Caucasian Z 11   Orthodox 4
Mixed Race 12
                R/C 3   Jewish 2
RELIGION (specify)   Sikh 5   Muslim 6
                None 7   Other 8   **G.P. CODE**

CWRC MRO 32 WRG 254

PERSONAL / MEDICAL / SURGICAL HISTORY

Medical and surgical disorders

T+A^s as a child.

General Anaesthetics

yes - no problems

Allergies

often gets a body rash ? allergy

Drugs taken in pregnancy
before first consultation

no

Blood transfusions

no

Alcohol consumption
since conception

YES	NO	N/K
	✓	

Family history
(especially cardio-vascular
disorder)

no

Smokes

YES	NO
	✓

BLOOD GROUP ?			
1 O Pos	4 A Pos	7 B Pos	10 AB Pos
2 O Neg	5 A Neg	8 B Neg	11 AB Neg
3 O Du	6 A Du	9 B Du	12 AB Du

Family history of
congenital malformation

no

Probable genotype

Recent Dental Examination?

yes

ATYPICAL ANTIBODY

HUSBAND'S GROUP	Genotype	B.T.S. Ref. No:	B.T.S. Ref. No:

NON-OBSTETRIC DISORDERS PRESENT **BEFORE** THIS PREGNANCY		NONE	1
Chronic hypertension (>−/90 before 20/52)	38	Superficial thrombophlebitis	11	Serious viral infection	23
Kidney disease	2	THROMBOEMBOLISM	12	Tropical infestation	25
Urinary infection (growth on M.S.U.)	39	ANTICOAGULATION	14	Proven venereal infection	26
Other urinary tract disorder	3	Autoimmune disorder	16	Epilepsy	27
Abnormal glucose tolerance test	4	Allergy	17	Other neurological disorder	28
Renal glycosuria	5	BLOOD TRANSFUSION	18	Musculoskeletal	29
Thyroid disease	6	Transfusion reaction	19	Psychiatric	30
Other endocrine disease (excl. gynaecological)	7	Skin	20	Breast disease	32
Gastrointestinal tract disorder	8	Haemoglobinopathy	41	Malignant disease	33
Heart disease (proven on investigation)	9	Other blood disorder (excl. defic. anaemia)	21	Liver disease	34
Chronic respiratory disease	40	Tuberculosis	22		42

PREVIOUS PREGNANCIES

Date	Gest. age	Place	Complications	Birth weight	Sex	Health now
			Primigravida.			

Number of existing children living with patient (incl. adopted in)

Number of livebirths after 28/52		Number of stillbirths	
Number of livebirths before 28/52		Number of babies with non-lethal congenital malformations	
Number of neonatal deaths		Number of babies with lethal congenital malformations	
Number of multiple pregnancies		Number of vaginal T.O.P.s — surgical	
Number of miscarriages before 14/52		Number of vaginal T.O.P.s — drug induced	
Number of miscarriages 14 – 19/52		Number of hysterotomies	
Number of miscarriages after 20/52		Number of babies dying of obstetric or neonatal cause	

GYNAECOLOGICAL HISTORY

no

No gynaecological history		
Abnormal Cervical Cytology		
Investigated infertility		
Surgery to treat infertility		
Drugs to treat defective ovulation		
Male factor		
A.I.D.		
Scarred uterus	In pregnancy	
Scarred cervix	In pregnancy	
Other gynaecological disease		

Date of last Cervical Cytology *never had one*

CLINICAL DETAILS

REFERRAL NO ▮▮▮▮▮ CONSULTANT......   DATE ▮▮▮▮▮▮▮

PATIENT NAME   DOB ▮▮▮▮▮▮▮

DIAGNOSTIC .... DATE .... UNIT .... INVESTIGATION ....

TESTS .... DATE .... UNIT .... INVESTIGATION ....

.... DATE .... UNIT .... INVESTIGATION ....

CURRENT MEDICATION ....

REASON FOR REFERRAL   16.6.98

Dear

Jennifer Elliott,
NHS No

Referral reason - routine ante natal booking.

This pleasant 17 year old girl finds herself unexpectedly pregnant by her boyfriend with whom she has had a long standing relationship. Her last period, we believe, was mid to late March but she has had irregular periods for the past 8 months or so since coming off the combined oral contraceptive pill.

On discussion with her mother and herself, there appear to be no underlying significant medical or family obstetric factors and I have commenced her on Folic Acid prophylaxis and will be willing to share the care in the usual manner.

Kind regards.

Yours sincerely,

SIGNATURE ....

REFERRING GP NAME ....

PRACTICE STAMP

                                           CODE ▮▮▮▮▮▮▮▮

My memories of the scan are vague. I remember I saw some blobs on the screen we were shown at the end of the scan but I have to admit, I wasn't sure what I was looking at! However, all seemed well with my precious baby.

9 July 1998

Clinic 8 July 1998

Dear

Jennifer ELLIOTT dob:

LMP: 7 March 1998   **EDD:** 26 December 1998 (By Scan)

I booked Jennifer under my antenatal care this afternoon. She is now 15 weeks and 4 days in her first pregnancy, and everything appears to be progressing normally. She is going to see our social worker, she is just a 6th former at school at the moment.

She has accepted my offer of an 18 week scan, and if that is normal, I would like to share her care in the usual way, with us seeing her at 36 and 41 weeks' gestation.

Yours sincerely

Reader/Honorary Consultant in
Obstetrics and Gynaecology

cc   Midwives

Leeds City Council & Leeds Hospitals
Initial Assessment - Children   *JGT*

Social Work Referral Form   WVG081

PERSONAL DETAILS
SSD No... .... Hospital/Team... *C W* .... Already Known Yes ☐ No ☑
Last Name... *Elliot* .... First Name(s)... *Jennifer*
Gender M ☐ F ☑ Date of Birth............... Approximate Age *(if DOB unknown)* *17*

ADDRESS	**GP DETAILS**
Flat No.......... House/Flat Name..............	Name ....
	Practice ....
House No. Street.....	Address ....
District... .. City.. *Leeds*	....
Postcode........ Tel............	Postcode......

ETHNICITY   **USER GROUP**

Caucasian

Preferred Language...........	☐ 001 Physical Illness ☐ 011 Mental Illness
Religion...........	☐ 021 Learning Disability ☐ 031 Physical Disability
	☐ 041 Sensory Impaired ☐ 099 Other/None

FAMILY COMPOSITION   **MEDICAL DETAILS OF CHILD** *(relevant to referral)*
(include relationship to referred child)

Mother -   *Pregnant*

Family Nursery Centre or School Attended

Persons Already Involved - please identify job title, agency and contact point
1 .... *Referred by Antenatal.* ....
2 ....
3 ....

PATIENT DETAILS
Admission Date.. *8/7/98* ..... In-patient ☐ Out-patient ☑ Medical No ....
Consultant..... .... Ward. *Antenatal* ..... Discharge Date ....

REFERRAL DETAILS   Date. *8/7/98* ..... Time.. *pm* ....
REFERRAL AGENT *Anke natal* ..... Tel. *2923 3* ... Feedback Required? Yes ☐ No ☐
REFERRAL   ☐ 001 Visit to Office   ☐ 002 Telephone   ☐ 003 Letter
METHOD   ☐ 004 Fax   ☐ 005 Electronic Mail ☑ 006 Nursing Staff Completed Form

REFERRAL REASONS - Please tick all reasons that you are aware of, then circle the most important *up* to a maximum of three

☐ 231 Adult to adult abuse	☑ 111 Finance	☐ 211 Parenting Support
☐ 223 Suspected Emotional Abuse*	☐ 201 Child Behaviour	☐ 101 Housing Accommodation
☐ 061 Physical Health	☐ 222 Suspected Neglect*	☐ 021 Domestic Activities
☐ 071 Learning/Work/Leisure	☐ 052 Substance Misuse	☐ 221 Suspected Physical/Sexual
☐ 051 Emotional/Mental Health	☐ 011 Mobility	Abuse*
☐ 001 Personal Care	☐ 241 Youth Justice	☐ 199 Other *(please specify)*

Note *Indicates that a Child Protection Monitoring Form should begin at this point*   PTO

**PINK AND WHITE COPIES STAY AT SOCIAL WORK DEPARTMENT.
BLUE COPY TO BE RETAINED ON MEDICAL NOTES**

I was referred to Social Services because of my age. I agreed to see the social worker for advice on financial support and my education. Reece and I would both still be at school when our baby was due, so we were told it was going to be hard financially. I wasn't too worried. We were extremely lucky because my mum and dad were able to house and support us. They even moved out of their double bedroom into the smaller one as Reece and I would be able to fit a cot in the bigger one. Things were going well and I was positive about our future as a family.

Thankfully, Reece's dad had come to accept the pregnancy. We had been to speak to him and reassure him that it wasn't the end of either of our educational journeys (although I wasn't bothered if was the end of mine!). I was living a quiet life and not really spending time with my friends, as they were all still going out and enjoying drinking and smoking. Everyone had started going to the pub now, rather than the park, but I just wasn't interested. This was at the time of the World Cup 1998 and my mum, dad and sisters and I would sit and watch the matches together as a family. Reece would spend some time out with his friends and then come home to my mum's with treats for me. I was craving Lilt, bacon Wheat Crunchies and Terry's Chocolate Orange. Things were progressing well with the pregnancy and I had a very small bump starting to show. With having no experience of pregnancy and no google to consult, I didn't have any reason to worry and felt content.

My next scan was on 20th of August 1998. It had been six weeks since my last scan. In the letter dated 8th of July 1998 it states that I had been requested to have a scan at 18 weeks but when I eventually had this scan, I was now around 21 weeks pregnant. I'm not sure why the 18-week scan didn't happen, although my grandad died suddenly the week before my scan had been due, so perhaps it was because of this. His death was very sudden and he was quite young and reasonably fit, so it was quite a shock for my family when this happened. I wasn't very close to my grandad but I will never forget the distressed noise my mum made when she took the phone call in the middle of night. My mum had lost her dad and I was heartbroken for her.

When I finally had the scan at 21 weeks pregnant, it was a very stressful occasion. I have vague memories and sometimes have horrific flashbacks from this time in my life. The feelings that resonate within me from around this time come from my heart and bring back painful memories. As we sat in the waiting room, pregnant mums came in, went for their scans, and came out smiling with their scan pictures. At my scan, the baby was in an awkward position and they couldn't get a good view. I was told to go and eat some chocolate and drink pop, as sugar might wake the baby and make it move into a better position. I hadn't felt much movement at all so far in the pregnancy but this hadn't concerned me.

The final time they scanned me that day, it was getting late. We had been in and out of the waiting room since the morning. Reece and I were due to go back to school after the scan but we had been there hours. I was getting concerned. I wasn't sure why. I just had a bad feeling that this wasn't standard procedure. Soon after, I was told that I'd need to come back for another scan at a later date, but first the consultant wanted to see me before I could go home.

The consultant broke the news to us that they had found a Nuchal Cyst and a Ventricular Septal Defect. I didn't have clue what these terms meant and had to have it all explained simply. I still didn't understand the implications. Essentially a Nuchal Cyst suggested that the baby could have Down's syndrome and the Ventricular Septal Defect was a heart problem. They arranged for me to have a baby heart scan. The results of this test were available straight away. They officially diagnosed the defect but the medical team were all rather positive about the outcome. The baby would need an operation but, if there were no other serious abnormalities picked up at a later scan, this would be a simple procedure to rectify and the procedure had very low surgical mortality.

My head was in a whirl. I then went for blood tests and an Amniocentesis that would determine whether my baby had Down's syndrome or another chromosome disorder. During the Amniocentesis, a long thin needle is inserted into the womb to obtain Amniotic fluid so that this can be tested. There is always a risk of spontaneous miscarriage after the procedure, so it was extremely worrying for me to have to go through this. The consultant said they would ring with news, hopefully the next day.

Clinic: 20 August 1998
27 August 1998

Dear

Jennifer ELLIOTT DOB

Further to my letter of 9 July Jennifer's routine scan has shown a nuchal cyst and the cardiac scan has shown a ventriculo-septal defect. The remainder of the anatomy scan appears to be normal. Prognosis for the VSD is good so long as there are no other abnormalities. I have performed a chorionic villus sample and hope to let her have the result by telephone tomorrow.

With kind regards.

Yours sincerely,

**Reader/Honorary Consultant in
Obstetrics and Gynaecology**

Hospital No:	Source: LGI	Cons:
Surname: ELLIOTT	Address:	G.P.
Forenames: JENNIFER		
D.O.B.:		
BTS Number:		

Group: O Rh(D) POSITIVE   ANTIBODY SCREEN : NEGATIVE

Laboratory Comment: STS Negative

16 JUL 1998

Authorised:	Date: 10/7/98	Sample No:

NATIONAL BLOOD SERVICE –
Bridle Path, LEEDS LS15 7TW   Tel. 0113 2148600

ANTENATAL SEROLOGY

TEAR OFF FORM BELOW FOR NEXT REQUEST

REPEAT ANTENATAL REQUEST FORM

Hospital No:	D.O.B.:	BTS No.:
Surname: ELLIOTT		
Forenames: JENNIFER		
Address:	Consultant/G.P.:	Report to be sent to:
	Hospital/Surgery:	
	EDD: 1/12/98	

Specimens Required: minimum 4 ml EDTA and 7 ml clotted

PLEASE ENSURE ALL SECTIONS ARE COMPLETED OR AMENDED AS NECESSARY		BTS use only
Amendments/Additional Information:	Private Patient: YES / NO	
Anti-D Immunoglobulin Injections in last 6 months: YES / NO Date Given:	History of Transfusion: YES / NO Date Given:	Date Sample Taken:

NATIONAL BLOOD SERVICE –
Bridle Path, LEEDS LS15 7TW   Tel. 0113 2148600

ANTENATAL SEROLOGY

49

Fetal Cardiology
Non Invasive Heart Unit
Yorkshire Heart Centre
E Floor, Leeds General Infirmary
Great George St
LS1 3EX
Tel: 01132 432799 Direct line: 0113 392 5757 Fax: 0113 392 5784

Dept. of Obstetrics and Gynaecology
Leeds General Infirmary
Great George Street
Leeds
LS1 3EX

Date: 20th August 1998

Patient : **Jennifer ELLIOTT**   Hosp No

Gestation: 21 weeks; Pregnancy Number: 1; Reason for referral: Nuchal thickeni
Referred by: LGI

FETAL ECHOCARDIOGRAM REPORT   Date of Scan: 20/08/98

Thankyou for referring this lady for detailed fetal echocardiography. She was 21 weeks into this her
first pregnancy, the reason for referral being a nuchal cyst.
The heart has four chambers with two normally connected great arteries and two atrioventricular
valves. There appears to be a defect in the inlet portion of the ventricular septum. If necessary this
would be repairable with a very low surgical mortality.

Yours sincerely

Consultant Paediatric Cardiologist

```
                        RADIOLOGY REPORT
        CLARENDON WING - X-RAY/ULTRASOUND DEPT Clarendon Wing,

Patient    : ELLIOTT Jennifer              DOB       :
PHI No     :                               Typist    :
Referred By:                               OP        : Obstetric Outpatients
Reported By:                               Report Date: 21/08/1998
Verified By:
Scanned By:

Report: Obstetric Ultrasound Scan                    , Visit Date: 20/08/1998

Fetus Id:    1    LMP Date:           Gestational Age:        weeks
                                                              days
No of Fetuses:   1
Viability: VIABLE                     Placental Site: ANTERIOR
Presentation: CEPHALIC                -Position:
Amniotic Fluid: NORMAL

Measurements :-
Biparietal diameter: 51 mm    21 Weeks  3  Days    Range -     Days
Femur Length:        29 mm    19 Weeks            Range -     Days
Head Circum:         177 mm   21 Weeks
Abdo Circum:         155 mm   21 Weeks

Umbilical Artery Ratio A/B:        :

Fetal Anatomy :-
Cranium: Seen        Face    : Seen    Spine  : Comments Limbs  : Seen
Diaphragm: Seen      Chest   : Seen    Heart  : Seen     Bladder: Seen
Stomach  : Seen      Kidneys : Comments Gender : Seen    Probable Sex:
Abdominal Wall:  Seen                  Cord   : Seen     - 3
Cerebellum:      mm   Nuchal Thickness:        mm

Fetal Wellbeing :-
Breathing:           Movements:               Tone :

Interventional :-
Amniocentesis:          CVB:              Cordocentesis:

Comments :-



ELLIOTT Jennifer                 Visit Date: 21/08/1998
Report: Obstetric Ultrasound Scan

RESCAN:

COMMENTS:

There is a small cystic hygroma measuring a maximum of 8 mm in diameter and
the bladder forward. The spine in the region of the
the bladder anteriorly.
with a smaller cystic component 4 mm. This is causing nuchal thickening.
There is a suggestion of a left pelvic kidney which appears to be pushing
The distal sacrum does not appear quite ossified. I am uncertain
whether this is due to a normal variation in ossification of the distal
spine, or whether this could represent a mild distal sacral agenesis. A
```

30.12.98

I left the hospital confused and exhausted. When I got home, I attempted explain to my mum what had been said. My mum is a very optimistic person and reassured me that they were probably just being cautious. I couldn't stop crying and when I tried to sleep, I could feel strong, almost cumbersome movements from my baby, who was for now safe and secure in my womb.

Things were difficult at home and everything was up in the air regarding the arrangements for my grandad's funeral. We lived over

200 miles away from my grandma and grandad at the time, so it was difficult for my mum to know what she should do for the best. She was worried about leaving me now, with everything being so stressful.

After waiting on tenterhooks for most of the next day, I received a very positive phone call. It was a lady from the hospital informing me that the test for Down's syndrome was negative and all chromosomes were normal. This news, on top of the outcome of yesterday's heart scan, all seemed very positive in terms of the outcome of my baby's health. The date for the new anatomy scan would be set soon but before she ended the call, she told me that she had been able to tell the sex of the baby from the blood test and asked me if I wanted to know. We hadn't wanted to find out the baby's sex; it wasn't particularly common to want to find out back then as the scanning equipment wasn't as reliable as it is now, and so we had decided to wait. I said "no". I wanted a surprise, even though it was tempting.

After the call, I broke down in front of my mum and dad. I can't describe the relief we all felt. My mum said she thought that my grandad was sending a sign that all was going to be okay now, and we were all full of positive vibes.

```
ST. JAMES'S CYTOGENETICS UNIT, ST. JAMES'S HOSPITAL, LEEDS, LS9 7TF
              ENQUIRIES DIRECT LINE (0113) 206 5419
                      FAX NO (0113) 206 5419

           CYTOGENETICS REPORT - CHORIONIC VILLUS SPECIMEN
           _____


    Surname              Date of Birth      Date of Sample      Unit No
    -------              -------------      --------------      -------
    ELLIOTT                                 20/08/98

    Other Names          Age                                    Lab No.
    -----------          ---                                    -------
    JENNIFER             17Y


    Clinical Summary
    ----------------
    ISOLATED VSD AND NUCHAL CYST.



    Report
    ------
    DIRECT ANALYSIS: Karyotype 46,XY (10 cells)
    CULTURED TISSUE: Karyotype 46,XY. G-banded analysis showed
    an apparently normal MALE pattern.




    Signed             Checked by                 Report Date
                                                  09/09/98

    Report Authorised By
    --------------------

Notes
1 The finding of an apparently normal chromosome pattern does not imply that the foetus will
necessarily be normal.
2 Chromosomal anomalies may occur which cannot always be recognised or be properly interpreted.
3 Occasionally maternal cells grow instead of foetal cells and their true origin not identified.


       CLARENDON WING
       LEEDS GENERAL INFIRMARY
       BELMONT GROVE
       LEEDS
       LS2 9NP
```

A memory that really stands out from this time was one night when Reece and I went to the new pub in Horsforth that our friends had started drinking at, which was called 'The Old Ball'. Things had now blown over after the incident with Steven and everyone was intrigued by and supportive of us having a baby. A girl from Horsforth who I knew quite well called Jem was out that night, too. She was a few years older than us and she and her boyfriend, Tom, had a baby when they were sixteen years old. Amy was a cute little girl; she was about three at this time. They lived in a council house and I thought how I desperately I wanted Reece and I to be settled in our own house with our baby. One of Reece's friends, Mark, was chatting with him and a few other lads. I wasn't drinking, obviously, but I the rest of the group had drunk quite a few. The boys decided to go around to Jem and Tom's place after the pub closed to carry on the party and so I went along and chatted to Jem. She was rubbing my tummy and getting all excited. I started to explain that our scan hadn't gone as well as we'd hoped and that the consultants had found a couple of problems with the baby. I was still confused about the heart condition myself but told her what I knew. I then heard Mark (who I didn't particularly get on with anyway) make a derogatory comment about the health of my baby. He said something along the lines of: "If it's got a hole in its' heart and other problems, it doesn't sound like it's going to live very long". It was the heartless way he said it that hurt me and the fact that he'd referred to my baby as 'it'! Mark would feature heavily in my life not long after this and that comment came back and bit him on the arse! Unfortunately though, I was also on the receiving end of the bite!

There was obviously not a huge concern from the hospital staff about the need for a follow up scan because there was a three week wait between my scan on the 20th of August and the following scan on the 10th of September. According to my scan dates, I was now 24 weeks and 4 days pregnant. At the scan, the radiographer found it difficult to get a good view again and I had a feeling that they were going to break more bad news to me. My body was shuffled around, my pelvis lifted and tilted. I was told to walk around, have a wee, get a drink… the list was endless. Eventually, they seemed to be content with the images that they had taken. Then there was more waiting around to see the consultant.

The consultant explained to Reece and me that they had found more abnormalities and that I needed to seriously consider my options. What did they mean? I was 24 weeks pregnant. I was over half way through my pregnancy and thanks to advances in medical science, my baby would have good chance of survival, if it were born today! I just didn't understand the seriousness of the situation. Mr. Brown explained that I should speak to my mum and come back with her the next morning. He said that my baby was very poorly and that if it survived to the end of my pregnancy, then the prognosis was that he or she would be severely handicapped. (This was one of the un-PC words that would not be used now… in one of the letters I received, they even used the word 'retarded!') I was devastated. The consultant explained in lay-man's terms that my baby had water/fluid on the brain, which causes swelling and pressure on the brain. The brain would need shunting. (I didn't understand what this meant but I didn't like the sound of it). The biggest thing he said that stuck in my mind was the point at which he said that my baby would probably not live until it was two years old. I went home traumatised… but this was only the start of it!

0113 392 6314 (Direct Line)
0113 392 6531 (Fax Number)
JGT/ML

10th September 1998
Clinic   10th September 1998

Dear

Jennifer ELLIOTT dob:

I am afraid we have some bad news with Jennifer. She had a follow-up scan today because the anatomy had not been completed last time, and this shows the baby to have a Dandy Walker variant posterior fossa cyst. The fourth ventricle is dilated and there is a partial cerebella vermis agenesis. As you know, the chromosomes have already been checked and are normal, but the baby also has a small VSD, nuchal cysts and a pelvic kidney.

It is difficult to give a clear prognosis in this situation, as some Dandy Walker babies develop normally, however, I think the prognosis is poor, and I have told Jennifer there is at least a 75% chance that this baby would be handicapped, and it will probably develop definite ventriculomegaly and require shunting at some stage. Naturally Jennifer is very shocked by this information.

She is going away to think about things with her boyfriend and to talk to her mum, and they are coming back to see me tomorrow at 10:30am. At 23 weeks, termination would have to involve a feticide.

Yours sincerely.

Dictated but not signed by

<u>Reader/Honorary Consultant in</u>
<u>Obstetrics and Gynaecology</u>

I must have gone back to the hospital with my mum, dad and Reece the following day. It is all a bit of a blur as days rolled into weeks so quickly at the time. The consultant spent a lot of time with us so that we could fully understand the situation and my mum asked lots of questions. He made it clear that if this was happening to a member of his family, he would be inclined to end the pregnancy. When he explained how the pregnancy would be terminated, I was almost physically sick. I thought that the worst that could possibly happen would be that they would put me to sleep. At least it would all be over when I woke up. This was not how it was going to happen, though. The procedure sounded horrendous. I shook uncontrollably and cried when he explained what I would have to go through. Labour would be induced and I would then have to give birth naturally to my deceased baby. How could I do this? I wouldn't be able to do it.

I wobbled over my decision so many times. My mum kept saying that I was young and would have all the time in the world to have another baby. Reece seemed to feel the same. His dad had spoken to him about some of the disabled children at his school and how devastating it can be for older parents to live with, never mind for two teenagers who lived at home and were still at school. I had to go through with ending my pregnancy, I had no choice. I was doing the kindest thing for my baby.

The following day I went to hospital for the start of the procedure. As I was over 23 weeks pregnant, there was a slight chance that my baby would be born alive, so they had to do something to help the baby pass away. The medical team had prepared an injection which would enter my stomach and puncture my baby's heart to ensure that I would have a stillbirth. I can't tell you how distressing I found this. I felt like I was about to faint or be sick whilst they performed the procedure. Soon after, I was sent home with the instruction to return to hospital the following morning to be induced into labour. Going home that day, knowing that my baby wasn't alive inside me anymore was the worst feeling in the world and I just couldn't believe I had to go back to hospital the next day to give birth. How would I ever explain to anyone what had happened? I didn't know anyone that had been through anything like this before. I felt so alone and a total failure. Why me? Why did my baby have to be so poorly? I laid in bed that night expecting the usual kicks that had developed into a pattern over the past couple of weeks. How was I ever going to be happy again? I cried myself into a fretful sleep.

The next morning, I was admitted to the Rosemary Suite. This is the ward you to go to if you know you are having a still birth. It is kept slightly separate from the main delivery suites. Still, I walked past several pregnant women and photographs of new-born babies swimming under water. I felt like I was drowning with every breath. My room was comfortable and looked like someone's bedroom, with pine furniture and a wardrobe. At around 10.00am I had a pessary inserted into my vagina to start my labour. I prayed that this wouldn't be too painful an experience. The baby would be quite small and I hoped the birth would be quick. I was scared and numb to what was happening to me and told the midwife that I didn't want to see my baby. I remember being very scared of what I would see, although I knew that sometimes the thought of something is worse than the reality. I just wanted to get it over with and go home so I could start getting back to normal.

As my labour progressed, the pain was unbearable. I was getting very distressed, so I was given what seemed like copious amounts of Diamorphine. It blocked the pain and made me feel relaxed and sleepy.

My mum was at one side of the bed and Reece was at the other. I had got to hospital at 9.00am and by 11.00pm after a day of wooziness and pain, I was starting to push.

At 11.20pm my baby boy's chest was born first, followed by the rest of his tiny body. I was relieved that it was over and that the physical pain had stopped. I felt that the mental pain was yet to arrive. Mr. Brown had reviewed my due date and decided that the original estimate was incorrect and documented the birth at 23 weeks and 6 days: just one day off being officially classed as a still birth. I wasn't required to register the birth and although I would have a funeral for my baby, it wouldn't be a legal procedure. That night, my mum and Reece slept alongside me and my dad arrived later and slept on the floor of the hospital bedroom.

The next morning, a lovely spritely midwife came into my room and said she thought it would be best for me if I saw my baby boy. We had decided the night before to call him Andrew. This was Reece's middle name and I told him that whatever happened between us in the future, by calling our son Andrew, he would always remember that our baby was a part of him.

I decided to see baby Andrew. He was in a tiny basket when the midwife brought him into the room. He had a blue hat on, and his face looked very dry and red. He wasn't as small as I thought he would be. I stroked him and cuddled him in the basket. I felt like I couldn't take him out of the basket because he might break. He was perfect. It was very emotional and I couldn't stop my tears from pouring.

Shortly after, I was given information on my after care and on how to arrange counselling and the funeral, and then told I could go home. I just wanted to carry my baby boy out of the hospital and take him home. But that was a distant dream now. I left hospital with a keep sake memory card with Andrew's hand and footprints on it. I didn't want to take the photographs with me but asked if they could be kept in my notes, just in case I decided I wanted them at a later date. The nurse said that was fine and told me that Polaroid's usually last up to ten years. That time frame seemed significant at the time and you will later find out why.

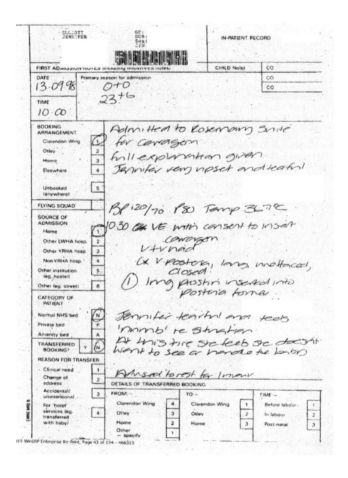

ANTENATAL NOTES (Continued)

11.40 Requesting analgesia. Tylex x 2 given
abdominal and back discomfort ++.

12.00 Called to see, distressed ++
not coping
Contractions palpated.
Advised to try on bath first, and
then for Diamorph if still required

12.10 Called to attend. vomiting ++
settled. Into the bath.

13.00 Settled.

13.30 VE to asses Cervix
VAV nad
(2) Cx no change, but pp felt to be Cephalic
at spines.
1mg Cervagem into posterio fornex.

15.00 Discussed with Mr Thornton
re discrepancy with dates.
further scan report (in transit) equates
to approx 23+6 therefore this is the
date we will work with

16.30 VE to assess Contractions consent.
Cx no change.
(3) 1mg Cervagem given into posterio fornex.
VE very painfull and difficult for ~~Beth~~
Jennifer, despite using Entonox.
Analgesia discussed for Diamorphine.

16.40 5mg diamorphine } im
10mgs maxalon }

SPECIAL LABOUR NOTES

17:50 Temp 37.7℃.
feeling cold. Anexon to observe.

19:45 ④ VE to assess cervix
cervix remains posterior beginning to
efface just admit a finger tip
Anexon Obs given
SROM✗a

20:55. SROM - Jennifer comfortable
backache only - analgesia not required
at present

21:30 Care handed over to change of shift
to A Furness + K Drummond

21:40 Jennifer very uncomfortable. Latest low
abdominal pain
1m Diamorphine / Sterp. given

13.9.98
22:00 Temp 37° Pulse 70. Jennifer is quite sleepy and relaxed at present ✓

22:30 VE by _____ ___ Jennifer consents -
Cervix extremely difficult to assess ___ ___ and ___
presenting part ___ below the level of the spines, ? parietal
part ? Cervix 0? 2cm dilated — is very
difficult examination for Jennifer + midwife.
⑤ Entonox given

22:50 Cared by Jennifer - experiencing rectal pressure
and an urge to push. Not inside Jennifer warns.
Entonox and encouraged to push.

23:10 Jennifer agrees to a Vaginal examination to see if
she is progressing with her labour — presenting part low.
Vaginal examination Pushing continued.

62

ANTENATAL OBSTETRIC COMPLICATIONS

INTRAUTERINE DEATH (before labour)	2	HYPERTENSION (see below)	21	X-RAY — abdomen	40
MATERNAL DEATH	3	PROTEINURIA (more than 100mg/L)	22	X-RAY — pelvis	41
HYPEREMESIS (admitted to hospital)	4	ADMITTED for observation	23	X-RAY — other	42
ABORTION — threatened	5	CONVULSION / FIT	24	CARDIOTOCOGRAPHY	43
— hydatidiform mole	6	Small for dates Suspected IUGR	25	— abnormal	44
— therapeutic termination	7	ANTEPARTUMHAEMORRHAGE — placental abruption	26	URINARY OESTROGENS	45
— other abortion	8	— evidence of coagulation failure	27	abnormal oestrogens (see below)	46
AMNIOCENTESIS — genetic	9	— indeterminate haemorrhage	28	OTHER FETO / PLACENTAL FUNCTION TEST	47
— Rhesus	10	PLACENTA PRAEVIA	29	ULTRASOUND (other than early routine)	48
—. lung maturity	11	MULTIPLE PREGNANCY	30	Other imaging technique	49
— other	12	Unstable lie (at term)	31	SURGERY — cervical circlage	50
BLOOD GROUP ANTIBODY	13	BREECH — flexed	32	— laparotomy / oscopy	51
— treated (including early delivery)	14	BREECH — extended	33	— other (specify)	52
— I.U.T.	15	BREECH — footling	34	PRETERM LABOUR (before 37/52)	53
— plasmaphoresis	16	BREECH — E.C.V.	35	Treated with uterine relaxants	54
ANAEMIA — less than 11.0 grams	17	Polyhydramnios	36	OTHER COMPLICATIONS (specify)	55
— megaloblastic	18	PREMATURE RUPTURE OF MEMBRANES	37	OTHER COMPLICATION (specify)	56
INFECTION — urinary tract	19	— vaginal infection (proven by HVS)	38		57
— intrauterine	20	— other infection	39	NONE	1

DRUGS TAKEN DURING PREGNANCY				Hypotensives	2
Antiemetics	3	Corticosteroids Immunosuppressives	8	Haematinics	13
Analgesics	4	PG synthetase inhibitors (including aspirin)	9	Antacids	14
Antibiotics	5	Cytotoxics	10	Other (specify)	15
Local Anaesthetics	6	Tranquilisers	11	Prostaglandin Pessaries	16
General Anaesthesia	7	Narcotics	12	NONE	1

DEFINITIONS

Pregnancy hypertension — B.P. $>$ - /90, or a rise of 20mm diastolic, on two readings. $>$ 24 hrs apart, in 2nd half of pregnancy.

Abnormal oestrogens — any reading (on full collection) lying below upper limit of borderline zone.

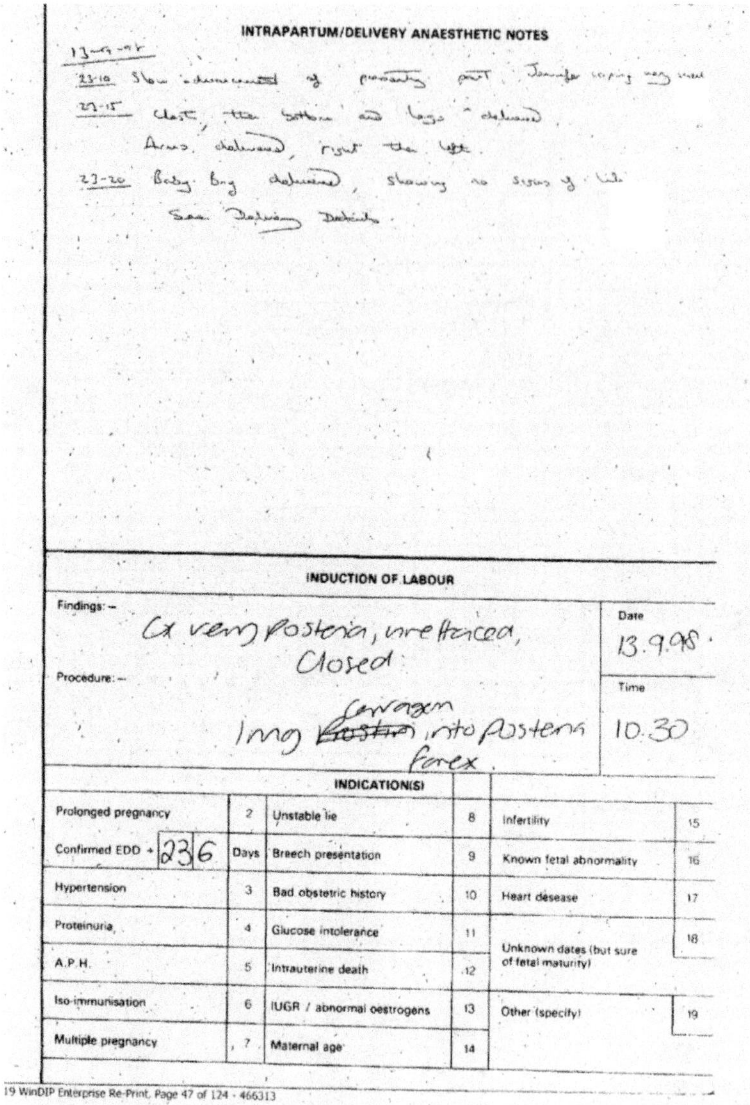

INTRAPARTUM/DELIVERY ANAESTHETIC NOTES

13-9-98
23-10 Slow advancement of presenting part. Jennifer coping very well
23-15 chest, then bottom and legs delivered.
Arms delivered, right then left.
23-20 Baby boy delivered, showing no signs of life.
See Delivery Details.

INDUCTION OF LABOUR

Findings: – Cx very posterior, uneffaced, closed

Date 13.9.98

Procedure: – 1mg ~~Boston~~ Cervagem into posterior fornix

Time 10.30

INDICATION(S)

Prolonged pregnancy	2	Unstable lie	8	Infertility	15
Confirmed EDD + 236	Days	Breech presentation	9	Known fetal abnormality	16
Hypertension	3	Bad obstetric history	10	Heart desease	17
Proteinuria	4	Glucose intolerance	11	Unknown dates (but sure of fetal maturity)	18
A.P.H.	5	Intrauterine death	12		
Iso-immunisation	6	IUGR / abnormal oestrogens	13	Other (specify)	19
Multiple pregnancy	7	Maternal age	14		

19 WinDIP Enterprise Re-Print, Page 47 of 124 - 466313

So, physically it was over. I went home with Reece and my parents. My mum and dad had taken some time off work to be there for me. I remember my sisters both being very upset and Gemma, the youngest, just starting high school. It must have been a tough time for all of my family. The next couple of weeks went by in a haze. My dad would go to the Coop near our house most days to buy Heinz tomato soup and crusty bread for lunch. I wasn't hugely weight conscious. I've always been slim but I needed to get back into my jeans before I could even think about going out with my friends or back to school. I also didn't feel like eating much, so soup was comforting and easy to swallow through the lump of pain in my throat. My boobs were so sore and even though I'd given me a tablet to stop the breast milk, it persisted and dripped from my nipples unwelcomingly. We had practical obstacle too - like a funeral to organise.

I buried my head in the sand in the days leading up to the funeral. My mum took me to buy a tiny wreath of flowers for the coffin and we also went to a local garden centre to find a tree of remembrance to plant in my parent's garden. I wouldn't have known what to do in terms of organising the funeral had it not been for my mum and dad. I wasn't sure whether to have a burial or cremation, I didn't know who to invite and just wanted it over. I wasn't sure how much more upset I could take.

I have no idea of the date of the funeral, which took place at Rawdon crematorium. I think it was around a week after Andrew died. In the end mum, dad, Reece and I were the only people present. We waited outside, none of us knowing what to expect. The funeral hearse eventually arrived and two very tall, smartly dressed men lifted the tiny white coffin into their arms and into the crematorium. This vision is a flashback that I have regularly. The magnitude of the occasion was so overwhelming that it took my breath away. We chose the song that I'd bought Reece on CD as a present whilst I was pregnant. It was 'Just the Two of Us' by Will Smith. It was a song about the bond between a dad and his son. As the song started, my tears felt like they would never end. I still get emotional whenever I hear that song. After a lot of thought, I decided to bring Andrew's ashes home and scatter them somewhere significant.

As well as help with the funeral, we were given an appointment with a grief counsellor. My dad gave us a lift to the hospital and in we went. I seemed to others to be holding everything together and felt like I was getting back to feeling normal. The counsellor's notes reflect this. I realise now that I didn't ever really consider Reece's feelings as my own were all encompassing. Looking back, I now know that it must have been an equally traumatising event for him. But as young lads often do, he either bottled things up or buried them and seemed to just want to get back to normal, too. So, as the weeks went on, we went back to school and kind of got back into the swing of everyday life. We had received an abundance of cards and flowers from friends and relatives with lovely words of condolence. I wasn't sure how to react to these. Going back into the real world and seeing people was a challenge but I was strong. Well that's what everyone was telling me, anyway.

There are two upsetting memories from this time that stick in my mind. Reece had gone out with his friends one night and I was staying in at my mum's. I was nagging him to come home and accusing him of abandoning me. Anyway, when he eventually turned up, he thought he had done the right thing and had brought me snacks. He bought me Lilt, Terry's Chocolate Orange and bacon Wheat Crunchies! How could he be so insensitive and thoughtless? I wasn't pregnant anymore! Why would I still want to eat these things?! I burst into tears and had a complete melt down in front of my mum and dad. Poor Reece. He probably thought he was doing a kind act. But no. In my hormonal mess, I couldn't see that and didn't speak to him for hours.

The second incident was when few of us had gone out to The Old Ball pub. I was able to drink again now, so was back on the wine and cigs! I was clearly determined to block out what had happened and get on with my life. We enjoyed the night and Reece and I went back to my mum's. My mum and dad's next-door neighbours had a new baby a few months previously and occasionally I could hear little Robert crying. On this particular night the combination of the noise from the crying, the alcohol and my still raging hormones was just too much and I broke down. Reece and I would never get to hear our baby boy cry or know what he sounded like. It felt so painful. I fell into an unsettled sleep. This would now be on-going occurrence. I had hoped that this nightmare was now coming to an end. Little did I know that this was just the beginning.

We collected Andrew's ashes and scattered them at the top of my mum and dad's garden. This was a very low-key event with just Reece and I. We planted the tree there, too. The garden is quite long and narrow and I've always found it peaceful up there. It will always be a special place for our family now.

We had an upcoming appointment on the 27th October, 6 weeks after Andrew had died. This appointment would be one of the last times we would visit the hospital for results and we were due to hear news of Andrew's post-mortem. We would hopefully get some answers about whether we had any genetic defects that could cause another baby to have severe abnormalities.

The consultant explained that the pattern of abnormalities could denote a syndrome of some type. For example, Andrew had an extra toe on each foot and this could indicate a genetic syndrome. Furthermore, they reassured us that after reviewing our family history and genetics results, they felt it was probably more of a sporadic occurrence. The plan was to send some of Andrew's post-mortem specimens off to London to check for Smith-Lemli-Opitz syndrome, this is rare and very serious genetic condition. This could determine the recurrence rate more accurately if a positive result. We were told that with the current information they had, the risk of recurrence in future pregnancies would be of 0-25%. Regular antenatal scans as well detailed anatomy scans would be performed for any of my future pregnancies. I felt reassured.

YORKSHIRE REGIONAL GENETICS SERVICE
DEPARTMENT OF CLINICAL GENETICS
St. James's University Hospital
Telephone No. 0113 206 5145 (direct line)

Our Ref:

Reader/Honorary Consultant Obstetrics &
Gynaecology   **Please quote on all correspondence**
Clarendon Wing
Leeds General Infirmary   Your Ref:

Date: 4 November 1998

Clinic: 27 October 1998

Dear

Re: Jennifer ELLIOT.

Reason fopr referral: **Multiple congenital abnormalities**
Termination at 23 weeks

Actions: **(1)Post-mortem**
(2)Discussed recurrence risks (0-25%)
(3)Specimen for Smith-Lemli-Opitz

I saw Jennifer and her partner at the prenatal clinic, this afternoon at the LGI and we discussed the finding of the post mortem which includes;

1.   Dandy Walker malformation

2.   Pelvic kidney

3.   Post axial polydactyly

4.   VSD

We discussed the possibility that this multiple abnormalities occurring in the absence of any family history could be a sporadic: In which the risk of recurrence would be very low: However, the pattern of the malformation can be explained by a couple of autosomal recessive syndromes, which would bring the risk of recurrence to 25%. Unfortunately, we can only test for one of them (Smith-Lemli-Opitz syndrome), and cannot determine which group they fall in at this present moment and hence their risk of recurrence at this present time is anything between 0 - 25%.

I am currently arranging for some post mortem specimens to be sent to London to be tested for Smith-Lemli-Opitz syndrome and we shall see them again when we

Cont/d

have the result. In the long term, we discussed that for future pregnancies we could perform regular antenatal scans as well as detailed anatomy and cardiac scans at the appropriate age.

Yours sincerely

Specialist Registrar in Clinical Genetics

cc:

YORKSHIRE REGIONAL GENETICS SERVICE
DEPARTMENT OF CLINICAL GENETICS
St. James's University Hospital
Telephone No. 0113 206 5145 (direct line)

Ms J Elliot

Our Ref:

Please quote on all correspondence

Your Ref:

Date: 4 November 1998

Clinic:

27 October 1998

Dear Ms Elliot

Thank you for coming to see me at the prenatal clinic at the LGI. You attended to discuss the findings from the post mortem and the risks for future pregnancies.

The post mortem was very useful in confirming the ultrasound findings as well as highlighting other abnormalities which we did not find. Undoubtedly, the decision for termination was correct as this child would have suffered from many problems and be severely mentally retarded as well as growth retarded.

With regard to the possibility of recurrence in future pregnancies, we are unable to determine precisely the cause of the abnormality at this present time and it is possible that all these abnormalities, in the absence of a family history may have occurred sporadically, in which case, the recurrence risk would be very low. However, the patten of abnormality that was found has been seen in a couple of known autosomal recessive syndromes in particular Smith-Lemli-Opitz and Trisomy 13. If these findings were due to autosomal recessive syndrome then in future pregnancies you would have a 1 in 4 risk of having a child with these abnormalities.

Each function in our bodies is controlled by a pair of genes, or genetic blueprint. These genes are inherited from our parents, one coming from each of them. When we have children ourselves, we only pass on one of each of our pair of genes to them and our partner does the same so that our children, again, have a pair of genes. In an autosomal recessive condition both of the pair of genes must be faulty for a person to develop the disorder. If a person has one faulty and one normal gene in a pair, they have no problems whatsoever.

As we are unable to determine which group you lie in then the risk of future pregnancies at this present moment would lie anything between 0 - 25%. We are able to test for one of these disorders(Smith-Lemli-Opitz) and I once I have the result of this I will send you a further appointment.

Cont/d

St. James's University Hospital, Beckett St., Leeds, LS9 7TF. Tel: (0113) 206 5145 Fax: (0113) 246 7090

UNITED LEEDS TEACHING HOSPITALS
NHS TRUST

ELLIOTT
JENNIFER

GP:
DOB:
Sex:
C/N

Clarendon Wing,
The General Infirmary at Leeds
Belmont Grove, Leeds LS2 9NS.
Telephone: (0113) - 2432799

14.9.98

Dear Dr

Delivery Details: *TOP for fetal abnormalities at 23weeks.* 13.9.98
Mode of Onset: *Cervagen × 5mg*
Length of Labour: *2hrs 30mins*
Mode of Delivery: *SVD*
Delivery of Placenta: *CCT complete*
Blood Loss (in ml): *150mls.*
Placenta Complete: *male - 640g*

Baby details:
Sex: Birth Weight:
Vital Status: LIVEBIRTH
Apgar score at 1 minute: Apgar score at 5 minutes:
Cord: Guthrie: Discharge Weight:
Length: Occipito Circ: Vitamin K:

Maternal Complications of Delivery and 24 hours post partum: Material:
          Removal:

Discharge Details:
Date of Discharge: 14.9.98
Contraceptive Intention: *Advised*
Follow Up: *Clarendon Wing Appointment. Six weeks to Send* *27/10/98 2pm*
Blood Group: *OPOS*
Puerperium Hb: —
Rubella: *immune*   Rubella Vaccine:
Anti-D: *not needed*   Anti-D Vaccine:

Yours sincerely

22 Sep 98. AT 0956   PAGE 1
              G E N E R A L   A U T O P S Y

ELLIOTT,Fetus Of Jen M

                    POST MORTEM EXAMINATION REPORT
                    =============================
                       Private and Confidential
                    =============================

                         Name : ELLIOTT Fetus Of Jennifer
                    Prev.name :
                      Address :

                Date of birth : 13 Sep 98
               Marital Status :
                   Consultant :
                         Ward : Clarendon wing
                     Hospital :

       Post Mortem performed on : 160998 at 1000
                            at : Leeds General Infirmary

       Post Mortem carried out with relatives' permission

                   Pathologist :

FURTHER INVESTIGATIONS: Chromosome Analysis, X Ray

PHOTOGRAPHS/VIDEO TAKEN: None

        Date and time of delivery : 130998 at 2320
          Gestational age by scan :   23
                   Death category : Therapeutic abortion
                  Weight at birth : 640.0
                      Dead weight : 570.0
                Crown rump length : 23.5
             Crown to heel length : 32.5
                 Left foot length : 4.2
                Right foot length : 4.2
             Circumference of head : 21.5

CLINICAL ABSTRACT

This was the first pregnancy of a 17 year old lady. The date of the LMP was
unsure (end of March 1998). A detailed anatomy scan on 20/8/98 showed a live
fetus with a BPD equivalent to 21 weeks. There was a cystic hygroma (0.8cm in
maximum width), and a small ventricular septal defect was identified. A pelvic
kidney was also present and a later scan on 10/9/98 showed a Dandy-Walker
posterior fossa cyst. A CVS on 20/8/98 showed a normal karyotype analysis.

Feticide was performed on 11/9/98 and she was admitted on 13/9/98 for a cervagem termination of pregnancy. A male fetus weighing 640g was delivered the same day at 2320 (23 weeks and 6 days by early scan)

AUTOPSY FINDINGS
....

EXTERNAL APPEARANCES
....

The body is that of a male fetus weighing 570g. The foot lengths are equivalent to 23 weeks' gestational age. There are signs of moderately severe maceration. The neck skin is somewhat lax and there are bilateral post-axial skin tags on both feet. No other external developmental anomaly is seen.

INTERNAL APPEARANCES (all organs show moderate autolytic changes)
....

RESPIRATORY SYSTEM
....

NASAL PASSAGES - patent.

EPIGLOTTIS, LARYNX, TRACHEA, MAIN BRONCHI, LUNGS - normal.

PLEURAL CAVITIES - both contain a small amount of blood-stained fluid.

CARDIOVASCULAR SYSTEM
....

PERICARDIAL CAVITY - contains a small amount of blood stained fluid.

HEART - there are bilateral superior venae cavae, the left draining into the right atrium via an enlarged coronary sinus. A small (0.2cm diameter) ventricular septal defect is noted just below the aortic valve. The heart is otherwise normal. The foramen ovale is valvular and the ductus arteriosus is patent.

AORTA - normal, apart from absence of the right umbilical artery.

INFERIOR VENA CAVA - normal.

NERVOUS SYSTEM
....

SKULL - normal; the bones of the skull vault are now partly detached.

DURA - normal.

BRAIN - this shows very marked softening. The cerebral hemispheres appear externally normal, with a gyral pattern consistent with around 24 weeks' gestational age. The olfactory bulbs are identified. The brain stem and cerebellum have become fragmented; a membranous structure is still attached to the brain stem and may represent part of the Dandy-Walker cyst, but it has not been possible to confirm the presence of this abnormality with certainty.

SPINAL CORD - not examined; there is no external evidence of a neural tube defect.

ALIMENTARY SYSTEM

```
22 Sep 98  AT  0956                                              PAGE   3
                    G E N E R A L   A U T O P S Y
. . . . . . . . . . . . . . . .
TONGUE, PALATE, OESOPHAGUS, STOMACH - normal.

INTESTINES - there is a complete malrotation, with a high mid-line attachment of
the mesentery to the posterior abdominal wall.

ANUS - normal.

LIVER, GALL-BLADDER, PANCREAS - normal.

PERITONEAL CAVITY - contains a small amount of blood-stained fluid.

UROGENITAL SYSTEM
. . . . . . . . . . . . . . . .
KIDNEYS AND URETERS - the right kidney and ureter are normal.  The left kidney
is situated in the pelvis in the mid-line and the left ureter is correspondingly
short.

BLADDER, URETHRA - normal.

TESTES - normal; found in the pelvic cavity.

EXTERNAL GENITALIA - normal male.

LYMPHORETICULAR SYSTEM
. . . . . . . . . . . . . . . . . . . .
THYMUS, SPLEEN - normal; there are two splenunculi at the tail of the pancreas.

ENDOCRINE SYSTEM
. . . . . . . . . . . . . .
PITUITARY - normal, not removed.

THYROID, ADRENALS - normal; the left adrenal is normally sited but is discoid
and attached to the lateral border of the vertebral column.

MUSCULOSKELETAL SYSTEM
. . . . . . . . . . . . . . . . . . . . .
No further abnormality seen.  The neck tissues are mildly oedematous, but no
subcutaneous cysts are identified.

PLACENTA
. . . . . . . .
This weighs 116g (trimmed) and shows normal fetal, maternal and cut surfaces.
The membranes are adequate and normal. - The umbilical cord measures 17.0cm in
length and has an eccentric insertion; two vessels only are seen on the cut
surface.

COMMENT
. . . . . . .
PROVISIONAL NECROPSY NOTE
. . . . . . . . . . . . . . . . . . . . . . .
This male fetus has foot length measurements equivalent to 23 weeks' gestational
age and shows moderately severe changes of maceration.  The neck skin is
slightly redundant.  There are multiple anomalies which include polydactyly,
bilateral superior venae cavae, a ventricular septal defect, a single umbilical
artery, intestinal malrotation and a left pelvic kidney.  Disintegration of the
brain stem and cerebellum has prevented confirmation of the presence of a Dandy-
```

On the 15th of April 1999, we had our final appointment at the genetics clinic. We were told that Andrew wasn't suffering from the syndrome that they had tested for but they suggested that there was a 0-25% risk of this happening again anyway. I was told to contact the department if we wanted a further scan in future pregnancies. It was very frustrating not to get a diagnosis but this did give me hope and I felt more optimistic that this could have been a one off, and not affect the viability of my future pregnancies.

YORKSHIRE REGIONAL GENETICS SERVICE
DEPARTMENT OF CLINICAL GENETICS
St. James's University Hospital
Telephone No. 0113 206 5145 (direct line)

Reader/Honorary Consultant Obstetrics &
Gynaecology
Clarendon Wing
Leeds General Infirmary

Our Ref:

Please quote on all correspondence

Your Ref:

Date: 5 May 1999
Clinic: **St. James's**
               15 April 1999

Dear

RE: Jennifer Elliot,

Problems: 1.   Multiple congenital abnormalities
            2.   Dandy walker malformations
            3.   Pelvis Kidney
            4.   Post-axial polydactyly
            5.   VSD

I saw this young couple in our Genetics Clinic. As you are aware, we have seen them in the past with regards to multiple congenital abnormalities. Given these findings, we felt that we ought to exclude Smith-Lemli-Opitz syndrome and I have not got the result of this which showed the 7 dehydrocholesterol was normal. I have informed Jennifer and her partner of this and I have told her that unfortunately, because of this we have not been able to alter their risks which were between 0-25%. I also informed them that we would not have any specific antenatal tests although given the nature of the congenital abnormalities, I offered them that in future pregnancy, we could do a fetal anatomy and cardiac scan. Should they want this, they should contact the Department in their next pregnancy.

Yours sincerely

Specialist Registrar in Clinical Genetics

St. James's University Hospital, Beckett St., Leeds, LS9 7TF. Tel. (0113) 206 5145 Fax: (0113) 246 7090

I promised my mum and Reece that I would give my body a rest and concentrate on my studying. I went back on the Pill for a very short time but only did this as I'd hoped to kick start my period into a more regular cycle. It didn't work, I was going six to eight weeks in between periods and I knew each time that I had zero pregnancy symptoms. Reece wanted to go out drinking a lot and was not at all interested in me falling pregnant again. He was spending a lot of time with his friends and even talking about going away to university. I couldn't even think about this! I just wanted to get back to trying to get pregnant. I was also enjoying drinking alcohol and going out, though, and I felt had some catching up to do. I would get in some horrible drunken states and always end up in tears. I wanted Reece to commit to me and I wanted us to get jobs and live together. We went to see a little flat at the bottom of Horsforth Town Street but Reece just wasn't ready for this. With the benefit of hindsight, I can totally understand why, now. What seventeen-year-old boy wants to grow up that quickly when he could be partying at university?

The Swedish students came to visit us later that month. Remember them? Yep, I had more or less forgotten them as well! I felt like it was a million years since our trip to Sweden. I was dreading the visit and I think the Swedish students ended up thinking I was weird and not liking me. They felt sorry for Reece because I was giving him a hard time. I got really drunk one night at my mum's house. She had made all of us a lovely meal and I drank far too much wine and ended up getting stuck trying to prove I could fit into a kitchen cupboard. Oh dear! My life felt a bit of a mess and I still wasn't yet an adult.

Reece and I seemed to be drifting further apart. I had started working in The Old Ball pub and really enjoyed it! I was still only seventeen but Steve and AJ (the licensees) turned a blind eye. We all drank in there and even went in for a pint on our lunch hour from school some days. We didn't need ID in those days. The pub turned into somewhere I spent a lot of my time, which in turn meant I spent less and less time with Reece. I had made friends with other girls who worked there and we had a good laugh.

We hung around with a lad called Phil who lived in one of the council houses on the estate. He smoked weed and never went to school but he was a nice lad and was part of our group. There was a group of older local men, probably all in their mid-twenties, who had a reputation for being drug users. Phil's brother was part of this group and a known heroin addict. The group could often be seen walking around Horsforth but they never came into the pub. They would get clean of heroin from time to time and you would see them out and about drinking.

Jack, a lad from that group started coming into the pub with his friend Nicki. He paid me lots of attention and I thought his smile was gorgeous. He looked well and confident. He would wind me up asking me what I was still doing with a 'loser' like Reece. I did think it was a bit rich coming from an ex-addict who had been to prison but hey ho! I was attracted to him from the moment I met him and each time he walked into the pub and smiled at me; I would melt. His mum lived over the road from the main shop we went to in Horsforth. She was an older mum and smoked like a chimney and chewed chewing gum at the same time, which I thought was funny and always remember. Jack was the youngest of five siblings and was known as the baby of the family. His family were working class and his siblings were mostly settled with children. What happened to baby Jack that he ended up an addict? I don't know. All could be forgiven with a look into those eyes, though.

Jack was now clean of drugs and lived with his brother. His family, and especially his dad, tried to keep him on the straight and narrow. Jack would ring the pub (we still didn't have mobile phones then!) when he knew I was working and ask if he could see me or take me out. Eventually, as Reece and I were clearly not going to be together anymore, I said "yes" and that night I ended up at his house. I had been drinking and we slept together. I really liked Jack and we saw each other a couple of times more. He even met my dad when he dropped me at home in his mum's car. (He seemed so mature, being able to drive.) God knows what my dad thought about a grown man bringing his seventeen-year-old daughter home! He probably just asked him what football team he supported(!) but I am not sure if he was completely clean of drugs during the time we saw each other as he was often elusive and seemed emotionally vacant with me. Then, Jack stopped coming to the pub and rumour was, he had gone back to taking heroin. I was really hurt.

I saw Jack sporadically over the next few years until he moved to Wales with his sister. He decided to move down to live with her because he would always be tempted to be on drugs whilst he lived in Horsforth. All of his friends were the same - on and off hard drugs and this was all he had known. He sent me a Facebook message years ago apologising for the way he treated me and telling me that it had been the drugs and subsequent depression that affected his behaviour. It was the best thing ever for Jack to move out of Horsforth. The last I heard, he was working with ex-drug users in Wales and was keeping fit running and walking in the beautiful welsh countryside. I am glad he's doing well for himself. I wish now that I'd had the courage at the time to leave Horsforth, too.

Things still were complicated with Reece but I was finding it hard to completely cut ties with him. We had been through a traumatic event together that had created a bond between us. I felt I didn't love him in the same way anymore, though and it was not fair to keep him hanging on.

Things then went from bad to worse for us. We tried to reconcile at Christmas when our baby would have been due. We spent time together and I have a memory of us going to see 'Spice World the Movie' when it first came out on Boxing Day at the Showcase cinema. Mel B was there with her family from Leeds. She was wearing a purple jumpsuit and people crowded around her for photographs and autographs. After a lovely Christmas together, Reece rang me just before new year to say he was in Amsterdam with his friend Sean. Sean was a member of the boy band '5ive'. With their newfound fame, they were travelling to London and abroad with the band. All I could think of was Reece and Sean being with all Sean's girly groupies when he should have been with me and our new baby. He later admitted he cheated on this trip. How could I be mad with him? I had been with Jack and really hurt him. It was as if our trauma had pushed us apart when we should have been closer.

Now I'm older, I understand that people handle grief in very different ways. We were teenagers and we just couldn't handle what we'd been through. I take full responsibility for our relationship finally breaking up, as I was the one who was unfaithful first. Reece was my first love, and I his. It was so sad that the emotions that came with the turmoil we'd experienced led us to do things we would not usually have done, in order to cope. Reece and I both have fond memories of our time together and will always have a unique bond because of the experience we shared.

I was now about to make another decision that would change my future forever.

Chapter 6: Mark

I finished school and was happy to have achieved a merit for my GNVQ. This is the equivalent of two B's at 'A' level in today's money. My family were delighted that I had completed the course and achieved such a good result. After the year I'd just had, I was proud of myself. I could have gone to University but needed to have two years' experience of working in a relevant setting in order to be able to apply for the social work course I wanted to study. Reece was due to go to Newcastle University. Deep down, I felt I didn't have the confidence to leave home after what I'd been through anyway and so was happy not to have that added pressure.

I decided to look for jobs closer to home instead. Luckily, an opportunity soon came up. Dad had taken early retirement from Roundhay High School and was doing regular long-term supply work at a high school for children with behavioural problems as well as some with mild learning difficulties. I have always had a strong social conscience and empathy for other people's welfare from a young age and had always been drawn to working with children, so when a teaching assistant role at the school was advertised, I applied and got the job.

It was a small school. The rules and regulations weren't as strict as in mainstream high schools, and expectations weren't as high either. We would take the children out on walks and bike rides. Some of the pupils could get very aggressive and uncooperative but most had been excluded from mainstream schools or were school refusers so this behaviour was to be expected. I felt ready to cope with it and enjoyed the challenge of working in this environment. I also loved the fact that my dad was there. It made me feel secure to know that he was around. The fact that he gave me a lift to and from work was an added bonus and meant we had time to chat every day, too.

My periods were still irregular and each time they came the pain was excruciating. I would flood regularly and bleed for over a week and I hated coming on my period because of the disruption it caused; not to mention because it signalled that I wasn't pregnant. My mum knew something wasn't right and when I chatted with my friends about periods, it seemed that on the whole, theirs were much lighter and almost pain free compared to mine. I could never just wear a tampon because I would leak out of it within minutes. I would be completely exhausted every month and I had to wear cumbersome night-time pads and 'period pants' as I called them. These were big belly warmer pants, which stopped me from leaking everywhere and I would also live in black trousers, just in case.

I started seeing a boy named Mark. The beginning of the relationship was a bit of a drama because things were still dragging on with Reece. We had been talking a lot and still met up from time to time, despite the distance with him now being away at university. I think we were both still clutching at straws and trying to keep things going between us, but far too much water had gone under the bridge by this point. My moving on with Mark hurt Reece even more because Mark was his friend. Why couldn't I make a fresh start with someone new instead of someone from the same group of lads I had being hanging around with for years?! I was just so insecure. I was pretty, with a good figure and probably could have had my pick of a line of decent men. I just felt so lost.

Do you remember earlier in the book when I told you about Mark making the derogatory remark about our baby when I was pregnant? This is him! Mark was a cheeky chappie who had lots of friends, although I had always felt quite awkward around him in the past and we had never really been friends. He was two years older than me and had just had his twenty-first birthday when we got together. When Mark was around sixteen and his older sister Katie was eighteen, his mum had left his dad and went to live with her partner. Their dad had now been with his partner, Jane for a few years and lived near York. Mark lived with his sister Katie in a small council flat in Horsforth. They'd had to move out of the family home when their mum left because the council needed to re-home a larger family in their house. It had been a traumatic time and Mark and Katie didn't have a good relationship with their mum, as they felt that she had abandoned them. As a result, Mark didn't really speak about his mum, and clammed up if I ever questioned him about her. When I started seeing him, he had recently split up with girl from Horsforth who he'd been seeing for a couple of years on and off and now more or less lived by himself, as Katie spent all of her time with her boyfriend at his place. Things moved quite quickly between us and I soon moved in with him. I loved the fact he had his own flat and I could really play 'house', funny, even in the early stages of our relationship, I worried about how I would cope with the stairs up to the flat, if and when we had a baby. Was it just me that thought like this? I seriously did have baby brain!

My dad would pick me up on the way to work every morning and then drop me off back at Mark's flat later. Mark worked for a print finishing company near Leeds and would work early or late shifts. When he was on an early shift, he would be up and gone for 6.00am and home for 2.00pm-ish. If he worked 'lates' he would start at 2.00pm and be home for 9.00pm-ish. Mark had a physically small frame but could eat a great deal and as I was quite a good cook, I soon realised that the way to a man's heart his through his belly. Of course, making big dinners to eat at 10.00pm was not doing my figure any good and I soon had to stop as it got to the point that I couldn't fit into my jeans anymore!

As a couple, Mark and I were a bit isolated at first. I think our friends were shocked and wondered what we were playing at by getting together. We had probably never even shown signs of liking each other before and some of them thought it was a bit 'offside' of Mark to start seeing me when he had been mates with Reece for so long. Mark played football with some of his work friends, and we had often spent Sunday afternoons in the pub with them after they had finished playing a game. Mark's sister, Katie was often there and we got on really well. She had also caused a bit of stir in the group by starting to go out with one of Mark's best friends. Remember Steven from the caravan? Yes, you have guessed it! Katie and Steven had been together a year or so by now and Mark and I started spending time with them and another good friend of mine, Diane and her boyfriend Tiger (Ty). Diane and I had been friends since primary school and she had been with Tiger since she was fifteen. He was a few years older but we don't mention that! Diane and Ty are still close friends of mine now and after splitting up for a couple of years, they now live together and have two children.

I never felt hugely secure in mine and Mark's relationship. He was a nasty drunk and I would dread us getting into an argument if he'd had too much to drink. It was horrible. I would cry, he would say hurtful things, and then in the morning he couldn't remember the row and it was like nothing had happened. He also smoked weed regularly. I smoked a bit very occasionally to join in but really didn't like the feeling it gave me. After smoking a tiny bit on one occasion I thought that there was a baby chicken in my fajita and was utterly terrified! The thought of smoking a joint on the balcony before work at 5.30am like Mark did every morning disgusted me. He was more chilled if he had smoked though, and we would have a laugh. I had taken the Pill for the first couple of months of us being together, as I knew this would kick-start my periods into being more regular and they wouldn't be as painful or heavy. That disruption was the last thing I needed at the start of a new relationship.

I came off the Pill around Christmas 2001. I had just turned twenty and would no longer be a teenage mum if I were to get pregnant. (In my eyes I would always be a teenage mum because of baby Andrew, though.) Mark and I had been together for a few months now and I was getting really desperate for a baby. Mark knew that I had lost Andrew but I hadn't really wanted to go into the details in any depth with him so far. I was trying to build a new life and had almost blocked everything that had happened from my thoughts and didn't want to bring it back to the forefront. It was hard for me even to say Andrew's name or to go up to the top of my mum's garden to see his tree anymore. I just didn't know how or what I should be feeling. A new baby would surely help: I needed to be pregnant again.

I saw my dad a lot at this point due to us working together but I wasn't seeing much of my mum or my sisters. I am not sure what my mum thought of Mark at first. I had moved out of home and into Mark's flat within a few weeks of us getting together and I got the feeling that she thought I was rushing into the relationship. On a positive note, she was pleased with me, as I had started to apply to study a course in youth and community development at Bradford College the following September. I had begun volunteering one night per week at the local youth club in Horsforth which I really enjoyed, too. If I did fall pregnant, I knew it would probably cause problems in terms of my accessing the course, but I would cross that bridge if and when I came to it. Mark and I were happy and settled and enjoyed our first Christmas together. I had a job that I loved, a flat to call home and a lovely boyfriend. I was happy but admit I did have pangs of sadness for Reece and hoped he was enjoying Christmas: our first one apart in four years.

In January and February 2002, I had normal periods. Not too heavy and on time. (Bliss!) Then when my period was due in late March, I started to look for signs and symptoms of the big P. No period came and my boobs hurt when I ran up the stairs to the flat. I was producing very white discharge, just like I'd had with Andrew, and was constantly starving. I didn't feel any morning sickness yet but knew that if I was pregnant, it was still very early days.

Now, one thing that I hadn't really accounted for was that my lovely boyfriend definitely didn't want to have a baby any time soon. I had talked to him about Andrew and he knew that I had always wanted to be a mum but the conversation hadn't really gone any further. When I told Mark that I thought I might be pregnant, just to test the water, his reaction actually scared me. There was no way he was having a baby! "We aren't ready!", "We have only been together a few months!", "You are applying for college!". And the list went on. It was unfair and presumptuous of me to have expected him to be happy about it but I had just assumed that with him being a bit older and having a good job, and his own flat, he would want a baby. It felt to me like a natural progression in my eyes, but clearly it wasn't in his! He asked me if I had been taking the Pill correctly. All of a sudden, I realised that he had been relying on me to take care of contraception when actually, I had been actively trying to get pregnant. Had he not cared or not noticed that my pill packet had disappeared from my bedside? His ambivalence toward contraception was just that and nothing more!

Anyway, a few days later Mark asked me if I had bought a test. I was so worried because this time I just knew I was pregnant. I put off taking the test for a few days and told him that I thought my period was coming. When I couldn't keep this up anymore, I did the test one morning before Mark went to work, and sure enough there were two pink lines on the test strip. When I told him the result, Mark stormed out of the flat and left me in tears. He told me to see my doctor and book an abortion as there was no way he wanted a baby. I was devasted. How could I have got this so wrong? If he had been clearer from the start, then perhaps I wouldn't have pursued things with him at all.

The following weekend we went out for a friend's twenty-first birthday in Headingley. Mark had made it clear that he would have nothing to do with me if I carried on with the pregnancy. On the night out, he bought me half a lager whenever he went to the bar. I kept leaving the drinks and buying crisps because I was insatiably hungry. He was nasty and ignored me all evening. I felt like telling him to 'piss off' and moving back to my mum's, but he had a hold over me and I really would have done anything for him. I loved him and didn't want to lose him. I didn't want to lose my baby either; but I was weak. I couldn't talk to my mum because she would have worried and would think I was stupid to even consider having a baby with someone who didn't want one. She would be especially concerned about the baby's health as well. Mark also tried the 'being lovely' act; telling me that if I had a termination, he would take me on holiday in a few months' time and we could try again for a baby in a couple of years when the time was 'right'.

Eventually and begrudgingly, I booked a doctor's appointment and we both went along to it. Mark did all the talking and I agreed to have a termination even though it went against everything I had always wanted. At the appointment, I was told to make a further appointment to have a scan at the abortion clinic to see how far into the pregnancy I was, and then, if all was ok, a date would be set for the termination. I couldn't stop crying. Mark was really kind to me after the long day and promised me the world: apart from having our baby!

The scan appointment was on the Monday. Mark had planned to go out with his dad and his sister for dinner on the Sunday. I was in such an emotional state that I didn't want him to leave me. He was trying to comfort me but also to get out of the door, as they were waiting for him outside in the car. Katie ended coming up to the flat to see me and I told her that I was pregnant. She tried to support me but said aborting the baby was probably the best thing to do because of the fact that we hadn't been together for long and we were still so young. I knew that her thoughts were rational but they were so far from how I felt at the time. I was left alone with my own conflicting thoughts while they went out to eat.

The next day, I told my dad that I was ill with a sickness bug and wouldn't be at work. When we arrived at the clinic, Mark was really caring and held my hand. I went in for the scan alone as men were not permitted into the room. I didn't see my baby as they don't show you the screen, but I told the nurse I was still thinking about what to do. I cried, and she held my hand. She explained that my pregnancy was at a very early stage and she could see a small sac but no heartbeat. I thought I was about seven weeks pregnant at this point but she said I was more like five weeks. She advised me to go away, have a think, and they would scan me in a week to check whether I was carrying a viable pregnancy.

I told Mark what I thought he would want to hear. He wasn't impressed that it would now be another week before anything could be done. My desperation to be a mum was increasing by the day and at this point I didn't think I could actually go through with the termination.

We went back to the clinic the next week. I sat nervously waiting for the scan. I didn't really feel pregnant anymore. I had never really felt sick, just hungry. (I have never told you this, Mark, so I am sorry if you read it!) I was told at this scan that the pregnancy was still the size of a five-week old sized sac and that the foetus wouldn't have progressed. I would most likely have miscarried any day. They decided to go with the original plan and performed a D&C (dilatation and curettage) on me at the appointment, which is a procedure to remove tissue or growths from the womb wall. And that was the end of the pregnancy. Mark took me home, bought me flowers and chocolates and we snuggled on the sofa. I thought he was so special and caring but looking back, he needed to be! I had just been through a general anaesthetic and was feeling hormonal and emotional. My world had fallen apart again.

I often wonder how that situation would have worked out if the pregnancy had been progressing well. Would I still have had a termination? The answer is probably 'yes' because I just couldn't see any other way out of the situation at the time. I was vulnerable and desperate to stay with Mark. If I knew then what I know now about the obstacles and pain I would go through after this experience, I would have grasped the opportunity to be a mum with both hands and never have even agreed to go to the clinic.

. . . .

Mark kept his promise and took me on holiday to Tenerife the following April. The weather was crap but we went out every night for meals and drinks and had lots of fun. Being away took my mind off things and I came back with a new sense of hope for the future.

September soon arrived and I started my course at Bradford College. Meeting a girl named Pam on my first day was a good start. I was still twenty and she was the same age. Pam had her own house, a boyfriend and a child. Her little girl was just a year old and was extremely cute. I was instantly jealous of Pam when she told me the story of her pregnancy and how she had become a mum. She hadn't even realised she was pregnant until she was around six months gone and then gave birth at nine months to a healthy and perfect little girl. Why couldn't this have happened to me? I was so frustrated.

I got my teeth into my studies. The modules of work were interesting and the other people on the course were friendly. We were a diverse bunch and it was fascinating getting to know everyone's motivations and life experiences. I was surrounded by kindred spirits and had a renewed energy about me. Pam and I were the youngest and became really close friends. Mark had passed his driving test by then and we had bought a little car with some of my student loan. He would drive me to college and pick me up if he wasn't working, as he didn't like me getting the bus from Bradford. My volunteering at youth club was going well and I ran my own teenage girls club on a Tuesday evening, too. We would look at magazines and discuss healthy body image and self-esteem issues, or get the nail varnish and make up out and chat whilst doing beauty makeovers. I'd just landed myself a new job as a (as yet unqualified) youth worker in the Youth Service, too. I'd be able to fit this in between studying and it felt like things were really starting to work out for me. It was coming up to Christmas again and I had lots to look forward to. I had passed my driving test, me and Mark were happier, and everything seemed to be falling into place. I felt sad that I wasn't pregnant though, and so despite all of this happiness, I started missing my pills again. I just couldn't fully embrace my life. It felt like there was a missing piece of me out there somewhere.

I started to pop the idea of having a baby into conversations with Mark and asked him whether he was ready to be a dad yet. He made a few vague comments about not being as disappointed if an accident happened. So of course, in my mind that gave me the green light to go full steam ahead and try properly for a baby. I stopped the Pill altogether at Christmas.

The previous summer we had bought a car from a local couple and the owner had kindly thrown into the deal a buy-one-get-one-free ticket to travel on a P&O Ferry to Dublin. It had been stuffed into a drawer for safe keeping and promptly forgotten about until after Christmas and when I found it again, we didn't have long left before it expired and so we booked to go on a last-minute trip the following March. Something else to look forward to! Me and Mark, Diane and Ty and Mark's sister Katie and her boyfriend Steven went on the trip together. We did some sightseeing, drank Guinness and had a brilliant weekend.

I had become closer and closer to Katie and probably spent more time with her than with Mark when we were away. I had always admired and aspired to be like Katie. When I met her, she drove a sporty little white car and she was very pretty, funny and popular. She had always worked in an office environment but dreamed of becoming a beautician. With my support, she applied to Bradford College to study Beauty Therapy. I loved this because I was her guinea pig for facial and pedicure practice. During this time, Katie and Steven and Di and Ty spent a lot of time at our flat and we often spent nights playing Monopoly or Scrabble, having a few drinks and eating a takeaway. The boys would often fall asleep in a drunken state, whilst Katie and I stayed up dancing and having 'heart to hearts' late into the night.

Anyway, back to Ireland. I woke up on the morning we left Dublin with a funny feeling in my belly.

Chapter 7: Jessie

Soon after we got back from Dublin, I went on two-week placement from college at a charitable organisation called BARCA. They support families and young people in West Leeds. I spent most of the time with the youth work team, and as I'd already been working two nights a week for the local youth service, I felt knowledgeable and comfortable and got great feedback from the other staff, which was a huge confidence boost. The youth work provision in the U.K has sadly diminished over the past ten years because of austerity and budget cuts, but back in 2002 the Government were throwing money into youth work in schools and into supporting outreach work on the streets. Sexual health and the prevention of teenage pregnancy was big on the agenda. The prevalence of teenage pregnancy in deprived areas meant that teenage mums were seen as a drain on society. The teenage pregnancy strategy had been a massive government policy in 1998 and money had dripped through to provide prevention work but also now to support teenage parents.

At BARCA we signed young people up to scheme called 'C card'. Participants were required to attend a condom demonstration and a subsequent chat with a youth worker about their sexual activity before being provided with free condoms. It was a good concept and really positive that young people weren't shy or embarrassed about using contraception, like me and my friends had been. Unfortunately, it did turn out to be quite a controversial approach though, as after the sessions we would often find condoms strewn around school grounds and local streets due to young people messing about and using them as water balloons!

BARCA asked me if I would do some paid sessional youth work for them, which I did a couple of times but I was too busy with college and my job to continue for long. I was also pregnant! We had been doing a pregnancy test training session at BARCA and I had a funny taste in my mouth and felt quite sick. I couldn't concentrate. Would I feel sick already? I must only be early? I hadn't done a test or told anyone my suspicions. I had felt tired after we had got back from Ireland but had completed my last week at BARCA and tried not to think about what the implications could be of me being pregnant. Would my baby be ok this time? Would the pregnancy develop? What would Mark's reaction be? I worried about my mum and dad and how much they would worry about the baby's health.

I was twenty-one now but felt much older. I also felt much more in control of my relationship with Mark. I openly told him I thought I was pregnant again and thankfully he wasn't too shocked. He knew it was what I wanted and I felt that he was secretly pleased as well. He had done a lot of growing up over the past year. The two pink lines showed quickly and brightly on the test. When we cooked our tea that night, Mark wouldn't let me eat some sausages that were going out of date that day. He said they might harm the baby. I knew then that this pregnancy was wanted, and I had the biggest smile on my face when I went to bed that night.

We decided not to tell anyone that I was pregnant until I had been for a twelve-week scan. I tried to be more open with Mark about my concerns over the pregnancy due to what I had been through with Andrew. I still found it very hard to talk about and when it came up, I would often just tell people that I had previously lost a baby, without going into detail about what had happened, and I often didn't mention it at all. I seemed to freeze when talking about it. I had been through a traumatic birth and forced to make a horrific decision to terminate the pregnancy at a late stage. I know now that it was perfectly normal to feel this way but at the time, I worried that people would people judge me. 'Walk a mile in someone else's shoes' is a common mantra of mine these days, but I wasn't the strong woman then that I am now.

I found it very difficult to keep the pregnancy a secret. I was physically sick most mornings and felt horrendously sick all day and night. The sickness was far worse than with Andrew. I would literally crawl to the kitchen to find food because I needed to eat to stop feeling sick, but my appetite was all over the place, so I never knew what I wanted to eat. Luckily, I had broken up from college for a few weeks and so I only had my youth work job to contend with. I took Katie with me for moral support when I went to see the doctor. I was very embarrassed when I had to explain that I hadn't been taking the Pill regularly and was pregnant again. I saw the same doctor as the previous year and I felt slightly judged by him. I worked with young people and advised them on contraception: I knew exactly what I was doing. (I must make it clear here that I would never have disclosed any of my feelings of my desire to have a baby to the young people I worked with. I was always very professional and have continued to hide my personal feelings about pregnancy at work.) At the appointment I was asked to give as much information about my pregnancy with Andrew as I could. I needed a lot of reassurance as I was extremely anxious.

CLINICAL DETAILS

REFERRAL NO _____ CONSULTANT _____ DATE [ ][ ][ ][ ][ ][ ][ ]

PATIENT NAME _____ I D ____ DOB [ ][ ][ ][ ][ ][ ][ ]

DIAGNOSTIC _____ DATE _____ UNIT _____ INVESTIGATION _____
TESTS
_____ DATE _____ UNIT _____ INVESTIGATION _____

_____ DATE _____ UNIT _____ INVESTIGATION _____

CURRENT MEDICATION _____

REASON FOR REFERRAL

Dear

Re: Jennifer Elliott. d.o.b.

30 APR 2002

A·S·A·P·

I would be most grateful if you could arrange to see this 21 year old lady, who is pregnant for the third time, as a result of an oral contraception failure.

Jennifer is happy to continue with the pregnancy, but is rather anxious as she had a pregnancy in 1998, for which she had to have a termination for gross fetal abnormalities at 23 weeks. At that stage she was seen in the clinical genetics department and I enclose a letter for your information.

Unfortunately, there is some uncertainty about her dates but it is likely that her last menstrual period was at the beginning of March.

I have today started her on Folic Acid and have advised her to give up her cigarettes.

I would be most grateful if you could see her in your antenatal booking clinic and would be happy to share in her care.

SIGNIFICANT (NOT ACTIVE) PROBLEMS
1986 Grommets inserted
1998 Legally induced abortion - TOP   :bilat.
:foetal abnormality
15.03.2001 Legally induced abortion - TOP

ACTIVE PROBLEMS
1993 Asthma   :treatment continues 2001
22.04.2002 Patient currently pregnant

PRESENT MEDICATION

SIGNATURE _____   Last Issue _____

REFERRING Acute Prescriptions   CODE [ ][ ][ ][ ][ ][ ]

Microgynon 30 Tablets   1 d   21*6 tablets   5.4.2002
Selenium Sulphide Shampoo 2.5 % 2 -3 week 150 ml   5.4.2002
PRACTICE ST Folic Acid Tablets 400 micrograms od 90 tablets   22.4.2002

Letter ✓
map ✓

Tues
1415h
1445

PRL 1

2010 WinDIP Enterprise...

I must have seen a midwife at least once but my memory is very vague and unfortunately my maternity notes from this pregnancy were missing from my medical records. I was extremely compliant in engaging with pregnancy services though and know I would have attended my antenatal appointments.

The first scan I had was with a Doctor Lynn Johnson on 14 May 2002. I was 9 weeks and 6 days gestation. I would go on to have a good relationship with Doctor Johnson. She was training to be a consultant in Foetal Medicine at the time and you could tell she was passionate about her work. Lynn was very reassuring. Everything looked healthy and positive, so after the appointment we went straight around to my mum and dads house and told them the news. I could tell that mum was apprehensive but we were all positive and hopeful for the future. My sisters were excited to be aunties and we all tried to put the memories of what had happened with Andrew behind us. We had been told that this baby had less than a 4% chance of having abnormalities and as Mark was a new partner, this percentage might be even lower.

Department of Feto maternal Medicine
Email:
Contact:
Tel:
Fax:
·Our Ref:
Your Ref:
Date: 7 June 2002 (clinic 28 May)

Dear

Jennifer ELLIOT dob

I saw Jennifer and her partner today at the Prenatal Clinic. As you know she has had a previous pregnancy affected by multiple abnormalities but has been given an overall recurrence risk of approximately 4%. On scan today there was a viable, intra-uterine, pregnancy in keeping with 12 weeks gestation. The anatomy was normal for this gestation.

She has a follow-up scan arranged for 18 weeks and also cardiac scan, and we will see her at that point.

Yours sincerely

Subspecialty Training Fellow in Feto maternal Medicine

cc

Consultant in Clinical Genetics
Department of Clinical Genetics
St James's University Hospital

The World Cup started at the end of May and brought with it painful memories of being pregnant with Andrew during the World Cup of 1998. The local pub had got a special licence to serve alcohol whilst showing the early morning games from Japan. While I was throwing up and struggling to function, Mark was going out at ridiculously early times of the morning with his friends to watch the football and coming home at 10.00am already drunk! Mark made it clear that he wanted the baby to be a boy, though after my previous experience I was just praying that this baby would be healthy and its sex was immaterial to me. I certainly didn't feel healthy due to the anxiety I felt over the pregnancy, but I was trying to eat well and remembering to take folic acid every day.

A couple of weeks later, I was back at the hospital being scanned by Lynn Johnson. Again, it was a positive scan and all looked to be normal and progressing well. I can't tell you how immensely relieved I felt. It is hard to find any words to describe my feelings on that day. I was delighted and we now started to tell friends and family that I was pregnant. We didn't have Facebook or any social media back then, so we 'rang' around our friends and the word soon spread. My friends at the Youth Service were pleased and the teenagers at the club were excited for me. One sweet girl even gave me some baby vests that her mum didn't use for her baby sister. The sickness and tiredness were gradually improving and I was up to date with my college work. Our baby was due on the 10th of December, so I planned to take some time off college around Christmas and then my family and Mark would help with caring for the baby when I went back to complete my course in the new year. I spoke to my tutors and they were confident that I was good student and would do all I could to finish the course. One of my mum's sayings that comes to mind while writing is: "Tell God your

plans and he will laugh at you.". I needed God and everyone else on
my side in the coming months.

Department of Feto maternal Medicine
Email:
Contact:
Tel:
Fax:
Our Ref:
Your Ref:
Date: 14 May 2002

Dear

Jennifer ELLIOT dob

I Jennifer along with her partner today at the Pre Natal Clinic. As you know, she has previously had a
pregnancy that was affected with multiple congenital abnormalities which resulted in a termination at 23
weeks. An exact diagnosis was not reached at that time. The baby had a Dandy Walker malformation, pelvic
kidney, post axial polydactyly and a ventriculo-septal defect. After discussion with the Geneticist we feel
that her overall risk of having a recurrence is in the order of about 4%. This is a new partner so her risk may
even be less than that. A scan today has confirmed a viable, intra-uterine pregnancy of 9 weeks and 6 days
gestation.

Jennifer is obviously very anxious about this pregnancy and therefore I have said that we would scan her
again when she is approximately 13 weeks to look at the fetal anatomy at that time. She will have an
anomaly scan scan carried out at 18-19 weeks and also a cardiac scan has been arranged. Hopefully these
will all be normal and the pregnancy will not have any problems. We will let you know the results in due
course.

Yours sincerely

Subspecialty Training Fellow in Feto maternal Medicine

cc
    Consultant in Clinical Genetics
    Department of Clinical Genetics
    St James's University Hospital

On the 9th of July I saw Mr. Simons, a consultant in Foetal Maternal Medicine. The scan brought back horrendous memories of a scan I'd had when I was pregnant with Andrew because the sonographers just couldn't get my baby in a good enough position to get a detailed scan of the head. This is obviously a part of the anatomy that they needed to see clearly, especially as Andrew had a brain abnormality. They eventually said that they wanted me to return for a further scan in two weeks. I was reassured that they had not seen anything to be concerned about and it was just that the baby hadn't been in the right position. Despite the reassurance, as time went on, I became more worried but Mark didn't seem to understand why. He kept saying that I should try and relax. As if that was going to happen!

Department of Feto maternal Medicine
Email:
Contact:
Tel:
Fax:
Our Ref:
Your Ref:
Date: 9 July 2002

Dear

Jennifer ELLIOT dob

I reviewed this lady in the clinic today for an ultrasound scan. Unfortunately the baby was not at all co-operative and we couldn't get any good views of the head. Although there was nothing obvious to suggest an anomaly, we feel that this examination is woefully inadequate and have arranged for her to come back for another scan when she is 20 weeks.

Kind regards.

Yours sincerely

Consultant in Feto maternal Medicine

It was a warm summer and I now had a small, neat bump. My bump seemed to show more this time than when I was pregnant with Andrew. I had been a little more self-conscious about my looks when I was pregnant four years previously, as I was still at school then and felt paranoid about my bump. This time was different. At the grand age of twenty-one I was secure and happy to look pregnant and was enjoying watching my baby fill and push out my belly. I bought lovely summer dresses from H&M and enjoyed showing my little bump off. I had started to feel some movements from the baby and would try to get Mark to feel them. He was very impatient though and babies don't ever seem to kick on demand!

Two weeks later, we were back at the hospital for the follow up scan and then for an appointment with Mr. Simons and Lynn Johnson. I remember feeling I was spending a lot of time at the Clarendon Wing again. It was all good though. At least they were keeping an eye on my precious baby.

But this scan was when the nightmare started.

There was another struggle to get a detailed anatomy scan. My baby was in a very awkward position, and in just the same way as it had happened with Andrew, it was a long and drawn out process and a very emotional day. The sonographer had very curly hair and was a pretty woman. Whilst she scanned me, she told me she remembered me from my scan when I was pregnant with Andrew. After four years I thought I must have a memorable face, or was it that my situation with Andrew was unusual? The scanning process seemed to last for hours, I kept asking if everything was okay. I was reassured they were just trying to get a certain image and as we looked at our baby on the screen, I tried desperately to believe that everything was alright but just couldn't focus and enjoy the moment. I needed to know what was wrong. My ears were ringing and my heart was palpitating. I was so anxious.

The sonographer wrote a lot of information down and passed it to me in a sealed envelope to give to Mr. Simons. The thought of what could be written within it terrified me. No one else got an envelope after their scan, just keepsake scan images to take home. I clung onto my scan pictures as we walked down the corridor to Mr. Simons' office.

Mr. Simons explained that they had not been able to see the baby's Corpus Callosum. This is a thick band of nerve tissue that separates the right and left hemispheres of the brain and allows separate communication between them. In cases where this is missing from the anatomy then cognitive, emotional, motor and perceptual aspects of a person can be affected. I had to research this again and again to fully understand what this abnormality would mean for my baby. As you can see in the letter, Mr. Simons said that this part of the anatomy can actually develop up 20 weeks into pregnancy, so this gave me some hope that there was still time for this to happen. Also, if this was an isolated abnormality, then the outcome could still be a positive one. He explained that there is a spectrum of outcomes for babies born with a missing Corpus Callosum. It can mean that the child can experience a mild learning delay but in worse cases it could mean a more severe intellectual disability. I couldn't take any of this information in at the time, though. I just wanted to run out of the hospital and escape somewhere.

Department of Feto maternal Medicine
Email:
Contact:
Tel:
Fax:
Our Ref:
Your Ref:
Date: 9 July 2002

Dear

Jennifer ELLIOT dob

I reviewed this lady in the clinic today for an ultrasound scan. Unfortunately the baby was not at all co-operative and we couldn't get any good views of the head. Although there was nothing obvious to suggest an anomaly, we feel that this examination is woefully inadequate and have arranged for her to come back for another scan when she is 20 weeks.

Kind regards.

Yours sincerely

Consultant in Feto maternal Medicine

Department of Feto maternal Medicine
Email:
Contact:
Tel:
Fax:
Our Ref:
Your Ref:
Date: 23 July 2002

JENNIFER

DOB:
Sex: F Ward:
C/N No.

Dear

Jennifer ELLIOT dob   Cons:

I reviewed this lady in the clinic today following a detailed anatomy scan. The scan has demonstrated what appears to be a normal looking baby that is appropriately grown. The only thing that we haven't seen clearly is the corpus callosum. This is not too unusual as the corpus callosum only develops at/around this time, therefore we have arranged to review her for a further scan in two weeks' time just to check on this but hopefully all will be well. In addition, Jennifer has a cardiac scan booked for Thursday of this week. Assuming all is well at that time I would be grateful if you could then share care in the usual way.

Kind regards.

Yours sincerely

Consultant in Feto maternal Medicine|

My next appointment would be for the foetal heart scan in two days' time. When I later thought back to the scan I'd just had, I remembered that the curly haired sonographer had asked me if I had a foetal heart scan booked. I thought she must have seen something and hadn't wanted to tell me. I doubt there is any truth in this but at the time I felt the whole world was against me and that medical personnel were holding the truth from us.

For the next two days I worried and panicked. I couldn't face telling my mum and dad until we had some firm evidence that something was wrong. Mark and I hadn't had a conversation about what we would do if our baby had serious abnormalities. I was hoping that we would never have to but I knew that this could be imminent now.

At the heart scan, the sonographer said that she needed to ask the consultant to come into the scanning room. They looked at different pictures and talked closely and quietly in a concentrated manner. I felt like shouting to them to tell me what was going on! What could they see/not see? We were ushered into a side room and handed a box of tissues. This was clearly a bad sign and I was already crying in anticipation. I had been here before. They told us our baby had a condition called Tetralogy of Fallot. This is combination of four congenital abnormalities which include a Ventricular Septal Defect (VSD) and a small Pulmonary Artery. They told us that our baby would be taken at birth and assessed for surgery.

Fetal Cardiology
Non Invasive Heart Unit
Yorkshire Heart Centre
(E Floor)Leeds General Infirmary
Great George Street, Leeds LS1 3EX
Tel: 01132 432799 Direct line: 0113 392 3631 Fax: 0113 392 5750

Our Ref:

Dept. of Feto Maternal Medicine
Leeds General Infirmary
Great George Street
Leeds
LS1 3EX

Dear

Patient :   **Jennifer ELLIOTT**
Hosp No

Gestation: 19 weeks weeks; Pregnancy Number: 2;
Reason for referral: Family Hist

FETAL ECHOCARDIOGRAM REPORT   **Date of Scan: 25/07/02**

Thankyou for referring jennifer for fetal echocardiography, the reason for referral being that she had a termination of her first pregnancy for multiple fetal abnormalities including a ventricular septal defect.

The scan today demonstrated a fetal heart with four normal sized heart chambers, but there is a ventricular septal defect with an overriding great artery. The second artery is small and appears to be the pulmonary artery. The pulmonary valve appears to be present, and overall appearences are consistent with a diagnosis of Tetralogy of Fallots or something similar. As such, the baby will need to be assessed by a paediatric cardiologist after delivery.

I have explained the findings of the scan to the parents, and discussed the possible outcomes and the type of surgery available for abnormalities of this nature. I am happy to see the parents for further counselling if they wish to discuss this further, or have any questions, and am also available on the telephone on the above number.

Yours sincerely,

Department of Feto maternal Medicine
Email:
Contact:
Tel:
Fax:
Our Ref:
Your Ref:
Date: 30 July 2002 (clinic 25 July)

Dear

Jennifer ELLIOT dob

I saw Jennifer today following her cardiac scan. The scan has shown that the baby has a Fallot of Tetralogy-type cardiac abnormality, with a VSD and small pulmonary artery. Dr Dickinson has seen her and counselled her about this, and he feels that surgical correction is possible with a good prognosis. Obviously, in view of Jennifer's previous termination for multiple abnormalities she is very, very anxious about this. I have tried to reassure her that this appears to be an isolated problem. She does have another scan booked in two weeks' time as in her last scan we were unable to identify the corpus callosum. I have reassured Jennifer that this is most likely to be due to the fact that the baby is only 20 weeks and that it is something that develops in the second trimester. I have asked   our Cardiac Liaison Nurse, to make contact with her, and we will continue to see her in the Fetal Medicine Unit for follow-up.

Yours sincerely

Subspecialty Training Fellow in Feto maternal Medicine

Department of Feto maternal Medicine
Email:
Contact:
Tel:
Fax:
Our Ref:
Your Ref:
Date: 30 July 2002

Ms Jennifer Elliott

Dear Jennifer

I have had an opportunity to contact the Cardiac Liaison Nurse. Her name is   and I have asked her to make contact with you, and she should be either phoning or writing to you in the near future.

I look forward to seeing you when you come back for another scan next week.

Yours sincerely

Subspecialty Training Fellow in Feto maternal Medicine

There were stars in my eyes my ears were ringing. I couldn't do this again! I just couldn't go through losing another baby. Why was this happening again? We were in the 4%. In my heart I now felt that the

Corpus Callosum wouldn't be there and that there would be another rare syndrome affecting my baby's heart and brain.

The heart issue, although scary, was a problem we could overcome. I could cope with operations, but I knew that I couldn't cope with having a baby with a syndrome that affected the brain and heart, with also the potential for further abnormalities to be diagnosed further along in the pregnancy. I felt I had made the right decision to terminate the pregnancy with Andrew as he would have been severely disabled and his life expectancy was to only reach early childhood. Was I now going to have to go through these agonising decisions again? I cried and cried for days. I finally decided to confide in my mum, as I desperately needed her optimism and reassurance. She told me to wait until I'd had the scan because nothing was certain and there was still time for the Corpus Callosum to develop. We all prayed that it would be present and show up on the scan.

....

On the 6th August 2002, we went back to our familiar home-from-home at the Clarendon Wing. I wasn't optimistic and Mark was now worried too. I laid there silently as they did the scan. I couldn't look at the screen and my breathing was all funny. The baby was in a better position and the scan was over and done with quickly. We then had our appointment with Lynn Johnson straight after. As I had predicted, they still couldn't see the Corpus Callosum and there was a slight pelvic dilation on the left side, which can indicate kidney problems. Andrew had this, and at the post-mortem his left kidney was shown to be in a lower position than it should have been. I'd had an Amniocentesis whilst I was pregnant with Andrew to check for chromosome abnormalities but the test results had been normal, despite him having several serious abnormalities. My hopes, therefore, weren't high that having the test again would shine further light on this situation. I agreed to do the test anyway. Some more prodding and poking was just what I needed! Lynn Johnson also arranged an MRI scan for the following Monday at Sheffield Teaching Hospital, in order to get some more detailed images of my baby.

Department of Feto maternal Medicine
Email:
Contact:
Tel:
Fax:
Our Ref:
Your Ref:
Date: 6 August 2002

Dear

Jennifer ELLIOTT dob

I reviewed Jennifer today following a further scan of her baby. As you know, the baby has been shown to have a Fallot's tetralogy. Previous scans have not confirmed the presence of a corpus callosum. A scan today confirmed normal growth, however we did not confirm the presence of a corpus callosum and the cavum septum pellucidum was not seen. The ventricles were within normal limits. There was very mild renal pelvic dilatation on the left side, and the previous known cardiac problem was already seen.

In the past we have been reassuring to Jennifer if this was an isolated Fallot's tetralogy. However, in view of a new abnormality I have discussed the possibility of karyotyping this baby and she has agreed to this. I have therefore made arrangements for her to come back tomorrow to have this done. I have also made an arrangement for her to have an MRI scan of the fetus done in Sheffield, which will hopefully be carried out next Monday. Once we have the results of this we will be hopefully be able to discuss the prognosis for this baby which obviously (if there is a combination of a brain and cardiac abnormality) may not be as optimistic as we have previously led Jennifer to believe.

I will let you know in due course the results of the further investigations.

Yours sincerely

Subspecialty Training Fellow in Feto maternal Medicine

Department of Feto maternal Medicine
Email:
Contact:
Tel:
Fax:
Our Ref:
Your Ref:
Date: 6 August 2002

Consultant Radiologist
Academic Department of Radiology
Floor C Royal Hallamshire Hospital
Glossop Road
SHEFFIELD
S10 2JF

Dear

Jennifer ELLIOTT dob

Home Telephone No.:
Mobile Telephone No.:

I have spoken to   about this lady on the phone, and many thanks for agreeing to perform an antenatal MRI scan. Jennifer has had a previous pregnancy terminated at 25 weeks for a baby with multiple abnormalities, a VSD, Dandy Walker malformation, a pelvic kidney and post-axial polydactyly. Unfortunately, no specific diagnosis was made and Jennifer overall was given a low recurrence risk. This pregnancy is with a new partner and she is now currently 22 weeks gestation. A cardiac scan has shown the baby to have a Fallot's tetralogy, but on scan today we have been unable to identify the corpus callosum and the cavum septum pellicidum was not identified. The lateral ventricles measure 9 and 10 mm, the baby has mild left renal pelvic dilatation and the previous cardiac abnormality is also present.

Previously we have been optimistic regarding the prognosis for this pregnancy, but obviously now we have a potential brain and cardiac abnormality. Jennifer will undergo karyotyping today and I am very grateful to you for performing an antenatal fetal MRI scan to confirm any underlying brain abnormality. Jennifer can be contacted at home on   or by mobile   . You can also contact me once you have the results of the scan on my mobile telephone number which is   or via   secretary on direct line number   .

Many thanks for your help with this case. We look forward to hearing the outcome.

Yours sincerely

Subspecialty Training Fellow in Feto maternal Medicine

To give Mark his credit, he came to every scan and every appointment with me. At Sheffield, I stood shaking like a leaf and trying to get my belly button ring out before I got inside the MRI machine. I hadn't been in one of these machines before and was very nervous. Inside, it was claustrophobic and cold. I laid there and prayed they would be able to see the missing Corpus Callosum using this more intricate machine. I just wanted to get home as quickly possible. I wished I was back at Clarendon Wing, just for some familiarity.

This was such a depressing and isolating time for me and Mark. His family were supportive, especially Katie, whose shoulder I cried on more than once. Mark was adamant that he didn't want to have a baby who could have be an underlying mental disability. I was so frightened of the unknown.

We were given the diagnosis straight after the MRI scan. It was the news I'd been expecting. By this time, I was used to bad news rolling in. Our baby had 'Total Agenesis of the Corpus Callosum'; meaning that there wasn't one there at all. Other abnormalities also came to light during the scan as well as confirmation of what we already knew was wrong with our baby.

My optimism had now completely faded away. I felt utterly depressed and the journey back from Sheffield was painful. I held my precious bump and cried all the way home. The atmosphere was slightly tense between me and Mark as I knew what his feelings would be now about continuing with the pregnancy. My heart was breaking.

THE UNIVERSITY OF SHEFFIELD

MAGNETIC RESONANCE IMAGING UNIT

MRI No
Hospital No
NHS No
Areas Scanned   Obstetric
Surname   ELLIOTT
Forename   Jennifer
Date Of Birth
Referring Hospital   Sheffield Teaching Hospitals NHS Trust
Consultant
Date of Scan   09-Aug-2002

Clinical: Known Fallot's tetralogy. ? agenesis of corpus callosum.

Technique: In utero protocol.

Report: Please note that this examination was performed for research purposes, the results of which should not be used to direct clinical management.

The MR examination shows complete agenesis of the corpus callosum but no other significant abnormality is shown. In particular there is no evidence of posterior fossa abnormality (in relation to the previous foetus' Dandy Walker malformation).

Conclusion: Agenesis of corpus callosum.

[*Report dictated by Professor*   *but issued unsigned in his absence*]

Professor (Radiology)

The Leeds Teaching Hospitals **NHS**

NHS Trust

Department of Feto Maternal Medicine

Appointments and enquiries: 0113 392 7172 (Direct Line) 0113 392 6531 (Fax)
Secretary to Mr Mason 0113 392 6829 (Direct Line)
Secretary to Dr Sparey / Dr Ferriman 0113 392 5144 (Direct Line)

C C File

Date: 07.08.2002
Hospital No

Thank you for referring your patient **Ms. Jennifer Elliott, DOB**

Indication: Fetal Anomaly: Agenesis Corpus Callosum; Fallots tetrology.
History: Maternal age: 21 years, (Rh D): positive.
EDD by ultrasound: 12.12.2002.
Gestational age: 21 weeks + 6 days
Anomaly Scan: Aloka. Transabdominal US. Fetal Measurements (plotted in relation to the normal mean ± 2 SDs).

Abdominal circumference (AC)	165.0	mm	⊢——◆——⊣
Femur Length (FL)	36.0	mm	⊢——◆——⊣

Heart action normal; fetal movements visible; cephalic; amniotic fluid: normal; Cord: 3 vessels.
Placenta: posterior, Grannum Grade 0.
Fetal anatomy: The following were visualised and appear normal for this stage of pregnancy *head, spine, neck and skin, chest, abdominal wall, gastro-intestinal tract, kidneys and bladder, extremities, skeleton*
The following structures were not examined at todays examination due to the gestational age of the fetus: *brain, face* .
Abnormal structures:
Heart: 4-Chamber view abnormal, Vessels abnormal; Fallots Tetralogy.

Amniocentesis Uncomplicated procedure, sample 15.0 ml clear yellow AF from 1 insertion(s). Fetal heartbeat seen after the procedure and the results will be available in 18 days time. The date for the patient to ring for the result is Monday August 26th on tel 0113 392 6588.

The placenta is posterior and unfortunately not accessible. We have therefore done an amniocentesis and will have some information available from this later this week.
Jennifer has an appointment for an MRI scan on Friday to look at the fetal brain and we will see her again after this to discuss the results both of the amniocentesis and the MRI scan.

Subspecialty training fellow in Feto Maternal Medicine
Consultant in Feto-maternal Medicine

c.c.   Ms. Jennifer Elliott
Clarendon Wing Leeds General Infirmary Belmont Grove Leeds LS2 9NS
Email: gerald.mason@leedsth.nhs.uk / colette.sparey@leedsth.nhs.uk / emma.ferriman@leedsth.nhs.uk

On the 7th August, we met with Lynn and a consultant in clinical genetics who I hadn't met before. I had seen a lovely genetics counsellor named Karen previously who had visited me at home and I had hoped it would be her again. Lynn explained said that they had now ruled out the major syndromes associated with missing chromosomes, but unfortunately, some of the cultures collected during testing had got infected and so they hadn't been able to obtain a full result. I was offered another Amniocentesis but I couldn't see the point in putting me and my baby through the procedure again, as we were now already aware of major brain and heart abnormalities. It was difficult for even the consultants to understand what was going on as this baby had completely different abnormalities present compared to Andrew, although predominantly both brain, heart and kidney related. We were completely confused and didn't really feel we'd gained any further information at this stage, when this was what we needed the most.

Until this appointment, we hadn't wanted to know our baby's sex. I just had it my head that I was having another boy because of the similar abnormalities. Lynn commented during the appointment that I had a different partner and that I was pregnant with a baby of a different sex. I was having a girl! This was a major shock and I burst into tears. Poor little mite! I thought about what kind of life she would have. Lynn then told me that with the heart problem she had, she wouldn't be able to carry children of her own and that she may not live long enough to even be able to try. I felt like my heart was being ripped out! What if she had the same intense feelings towards motherhood that I had and couldn't ever have a baby? My mind started racing, imagining the outcome for my baby girl. What if she had to use a wheelchair and had to endure multiple operations? We would all love her, I was sure of that, but was it fair of me to go ahead with the pregnancy?

Lynn was honest with us and warned us that other abnormities could potentially come to light further along in the pregnancy and our child could be severely disabled. She said they could offer me a termination right up to my due date.

I had so much to consider. I talked with my mum and tried to stay strong. She said she would support me if I wanted to continue with the pregnancy. My mum contacted a professor in London who was an expert in genetic abnormalities. He told her that if my baby had either the brain or heart condition, the prognosis would be much more positive. He considered this combination of abnormalities to be a rare syndrome that could have devasting results on the child's mental and physical development. I wish I could have looked into a crystal ball. I just wanted the kindest thing for my baby the thought of her being in pain was too much to bear.

Department of Feto maternal Medicine
Email:
Contact:
Tel:
Fax:
Our Ref:
Your Ref:
Date: 13 August 2002

Dear

Jennifer ELLIOTT dob

I saw Jennifer and with her partner today along with Dr   the Consultant Clinical Geneticist. As you are aware, Jennifer has had a previous pregnancy terminated at 25 weeks gestation for multiple abnormalities. The baby's karyotype at that time was normal male. She is now currently 22 weeks into her second pregnancy. This is a new partner. This baby is known to have a Fallot's tetralogy and an MRI scan last week confirmed complete agenesis of the corpus callosum but no other underlying brain abnormality. An amniocentesis was performed last week and the anuscreen has shown that there is no major chromosomal abnormality and no deletion of chromosome 22 associated with Di George syndrome. However, unfortunately the cultured cells have become infected with fungus and therefore we will not be able to get a long-term culture related to this.

We had a long discussion with Jennifer and her partner about the potential prognosis for her baby. We do know that agenesis of the corpus callosum can be present in normal people with no neurological developmental problems. However, it can be associated with a spectrum of learning difficulties and up to 10-15% can have severe long-term neuro-developmental problems. It is difficult to know whether the Fallot's tetralogy is related or whether there is a possibility of an underlying syndrome. Jennifer is aware that potentially, as the pregnancy progresses, some other abnormalities may come to light and in particular the baby may develop ventriculomegaly.

It is obviously very difficult for Jennifer and her partner to come to a decision as to how to proceed from here. Her partner feels that he does not want to have the risk of having a baby that has any degree of mental handicap, however Jennifer feels that she would find it very difficult to go through what she went through in her last pregnancy, as termination at this stage would involve a fetocide and induction of labour. She has support from her parents to continue with the pregnancy. She had contact previously with   and has asked to speak to her. Dr   has made contact with   and asked her to go out and talk to Jennifer.

She is obviously finding it very difficult to make a decision as to how to proceed from here. She has gone away from the clinic today to think about things. She has my number to contact me if she has any further questions. I have made her an appointment to come back to see   next week, however she may well phone and wish to be seen earlier, when she will be reviewed by   as I am going on holiday later on this week. I have discussed with her potentially repeating the amniocentesis, but even if this showed a normal karyotype this would not give any additional information to us in terms of being able to counsel her as to the long-term prognosis for the baby. Jennifer will let us know in due course whether she wishes to have a repeat amniocentesis performed.

Yours sincerely

Subspecialty Training Fellow in Feto maternal Medicine

125

Ending the pregnancy was a heart-breaking decision and one that a young couple should never have to make. It was going to be the hardest thing for me to do and the worst part was, I knew what was coming.

Department of Feto maternal Medicine
Email:
Contact:
Tel:
Fax:
Our Ref:
Your Ref:
Date: 20 August 2002

Dear

Jennifer ELLIOTT dob

I reviewed this lady in the clinic today for a fetocide, the indication being a congenital heart defect and agenesis of the corpus callosum at 22 weeks. Unfortunately the baby was in a dreadful position, lying spine uppermost, and the fetocide was extremely difficult. I did manage to get a sample from the heart which has been sent for karyotyping, as the amniocentesis last week for some unexplained reason was infected in all cultures. After this she was given 200 mgm of RU486 and I have arranged for her to come in tomorrow to the Delivery Suite for induction of labour.

Kind regards.

Yours sincerely

Consultant in Feto maternal Medicine

My mum and dad took my sisters away on holiday for the week, in order to give me and Mark some space and reduce the anguish for my sisters. I went into hospital once again for the procedure to put my baby to sleep.

Mark and his sister were my everything that week. It was strange not having my family with me and I knew that they would be suffering from afar. Going through this again was not fair on anyone. Labour was induced the next morning and was back in the same Rosemary Suite room I had stayed in four years earlier with Andrew; this time with a different partner and giving birth to a baby girl. During my labour, I asked if I could see the photographs of Andrew that were stored away in my medical notes. I desperately wanted to see him again. The midwife told me she didn't think that this would be a good idea. It probably wasn't. I was so messed up and hurting so badly, I just didn't know what to do and this came to mind as something that may help me.

I then remembered how bad the flash backs were after seeing and holding Andrew. I wasn't sure if I wanted to see or hold my baby girl, or even to name her. After a difficult and exhausting labour, I gave birth to Jessie Marie. Our baby was twenty-four weeks and six days gestation when she was born and so we were required by law to register her birth. I decided to name her after one of my favourite dolls from when I was a little girl. My perfect looking doll that didn't move or cry. Marie was Katie's middle name and I decided that she would take Mark's surname. Jessie was taken away and I was left in a lonely heap. I asked the midwife to take photographs and hand and footprints but I

127

told Mark that I would find it easier to get over this if I didn't see her. How wrong could I have been!

I was desperate to get out of the hospital. I had spent so much time there over the past few months. I needed to go home. I had bought new bed sheets and quilt cover as I knew from experience that I would be spending a lot of time recovering in bed. I also knew that I would find it hard to face the world for a while and so the thought of a comfortable bed with new sheets was some comfort. I asked the consultant for some medication to help me to sleep, in order to avoid potential flashbacks and once this was sorted, Mark took me home. This was the first time I had ever seen him cry. We cried together that night until there were no more tears.

ELLIOTT JENNIFER	GP: DOB: Sex: F Ward: C/N No.	IN-PATIENT RECORD
Cons:	‖‖‖‖‖‖‖‖‖‖‖‖‖‖‖‖‖	

FIRST ADMISSION NOTES (including MIDWIVES notes)		CHILD No(s)	CO

DATE	Primary reason for admission		CO
22|8|07			CO

Induction of labour at

TIME	
09·00	$24^{+4}/40$. P.0 +1 (TOP)

BOOKING ARRANGEMENT	
Clarendon Wing	1
Otley	2
Home	3
Elsewhere	4
Unbooked (anywhere)	5

FLYING SQUAD

SOURCE OF ADMISSION	
Home	①1
Other LWHA hosp.	2
Other YRHA hosp.	3
Non-YRHA hosp.	4
Other institution (eg. hostel)	5
Other (eg. street)	6

CATEGORY OF PATIENT	
Normal NHS bed	Ⓝ
Private bed	P
Amenity bed	A

TRANSFERRED BOOKING?	Y	N

REASON FOR TRANSFER	
Clinical need	1
Change of address	2
Accidental/ unintentional	3
For 'hotel' services (eg. transferred with baby)	4

Admitted to rosemary suite. Discussed proceedine has been in similar situation 4 years ago @ 23 /40, termination for multiple abnormalities. Is very anxious and upset. Her father has been informed by Jennifer (new partner) the proceedine and I have talked to them about what will happen today. has also discussed with them following a fetocide yesterday.

09.45 ①
100 mg Misoprostol given ℅ consent PV into posterior fornix. Will inform me of any abdominal pains and understands that Pain relief can be offered if required

12³⁰ Bloods obtained from Jennifer with consent. sent to appropriate labs

13⁴⁵ ② 2nd Misoprostol PV 100mg given ℅ consent PV to posterior fornix, os closed no change & uneffaced
2 x co/codamol given for 'bad period' type pains

DETAILS OF TRANSFERRED BOOKING

FROM:—		TO:—		TIME:—	
Clarendon Wing	4	Clarendon Wing	1	Before labour	1
Otley	3	Otley	2	In labour	2
Home	2	Home	3	Post natal	3
Other — specify	1				

Baby Brain

14·45 Diamorphine 5mgs given IM and Cyclazine 50mgs IM with consent. co/codamol given is not effective 'requesting more analgesia'. Period type pains are much worse.

16·00hrs Becoming more uncomfortable with pains are much stronger in back area. Would like more pain relief.
D/W   to discuss with anaesthetist.

16·40 PCAS set up for further pain relief. Feels pains aren't as regular as before but are more painful. On discussion with Jennifer she would like to have a Post mortem carried out, she's asking to have photos of Andrew, her last baby who was terminated, also photos to be given for this baby. She remembers we do foot prints and she and are undecided as to whether to spend time with the baby or to name her.

17·45 ③ 3rd dose Misoprostol given PV '/c consent. VTV=NAD, Cx effaced, os = 1cm dilated. Is much more comfortable with PCAS.

20·10 Feels warm, temp 38·1°C 100 mgs paracetamol given, fan in room, ice water to re-check Nil visible at perineum, Continues to use PCAS.
Pulse = 80bpm
21·00 Temp remains at 38·1°C

21·20hrs Dr
- At SR - Pyrexia 38·1°C
- Blood cultures taken + FBC.
- IV Abs + fluids.
S r/V male   #10 32/1

130

THE **LEEDS** TEACHING HOSPITALS	Information/Continuation Sheet	**1A** WWG105

ELLIOTT JENNIFER	GP: DOB: Sex: F Ward: C/N No.	Named Nurse .... Team .... Key Therapist ....
Cons:	‖‖‖‖‖‖‖‖‖‖‖‖‖‖‖‖	Team ....

Date, time		Signature
22/8/02		
21.25	Care taken over by M/w	
	Blood cultures have been taken (sent off)	
	Jennifer coping with pcas machine.	
21.40	Cephradine & metronidazole given I.V.	
22.05	Vaginal examination for misoprostol	
(4)	1cm dilated, cervix thick & posterior	
	100mg misoprostol given P.V.	
	Jennifer upset that she has not progressed yet tried	
	to reassure	
23/8/02		
00.05	Jennifer has started getting more regular contracting	
	Approximately 3-4:10.	
00.50	Jennifer continues to contract Moderate to palpate	
	In quite a bit of discomfort does not yet want	
	entonox.	
01.05	getting some pressure commenced entonox	
01.10	vertex visible	

131

ANTENATAL OBSTETRIC COMPLICATIONS

INTRAUTERINE DEATH (before labour)	2	HYPERTENSION (see below)	21	X-RAY — abdomen	40
MATERNAL DEATH	3	PROTEINURIA (more than 100mg/L)	22	X-RAY — pelvis	41
HYPEREMESIS (admitted to hospital)	4	ADMITTED for observation	23	X-RAY — other	42
ABORTION — threatened	5	CONVULSION / FIT	24	CARDIOTOCOGRAPHY	43
— hydatidiform mole	6	'Small for dates' Suspected IUGR	25	— abnormal	44
— therapeutic termination	7	ANTEPARTUM HAEMORRHAGE — placental abruption	26	URINARY OESTROGENS	45
— other abortion	8	— evidence of coagulation failure	27	abnormal oestrogens (see below)	46
AMNIOCENTESIS — genetic	9	— indeterminate haemorrhage	28	OTHER FETO / PLACENTAL FUNCTION TEST	47
— Rhesus	10	PLACENTA PRAEVIA	29	ULTRASOUND (other than early routine)	48
— lung maturity	11	MULTIPLE PREGNANCY	30	Other imaging technique	49
— other	12	Unstable lie (at term)	31	SURGERY — cervical circlage	50
BLOOD GROUP ANTIBODY	13	BREECH — flexed	32	— laparotomy / oscopy	51
— treated (including early delivery)	14	BREECH — extended	33	— other (specify)	52
— I.U.T.	15	BREECH — footling	34	PRETERM LABOUR (before 37/52)	53
— plasmaphoresis	16	BREECH — E.C.V.	35	Treated with uterine relaxants	54
ANAEMIA — less than 11.0 grams	17	Polyhydramnios	36	OTHER COMPLICATIONS (specify)	55
— megaloblastic	18	PREMATURE RUPTURE OF MEMBRANES	37	OTHER COMPLICATION (specify)	56
INFECTION — urinary tract	19	— vaginal infection (proven by HVS)	38		57
— intrauterine	20	— other infection	39	NONE	1

DRUGS TAKEN DURING PREGNANCY				Hypotensives	2
Antiemetics	3	Corticosteroids Immunosuppressives	8	Haematinics	13
Analgesics	4	PG synthetase inhibitors (including aspirin)	9	Antacids	14
Antibiotics	5	Cytotoxics	10	Other (specify)	15
Local Anaesthetics	6	Tranquilisers	11	Prostaglandin Pessaries	16
General Anaesthesia	7	Narcotics	12	NONE	1

DEFINITIONS

Pregnancy hypertension — B.P. $>$ -- /90, or a rise of 20mm diastolic, on two readings, $>$ 24 hrs apart, in 2nd half of pregnancy.

Abnormal oestrogens — any reading (on full collection) lying below upper limit of borderline zone.

POST-NATAL NOTES

PUERPERAL X-RAY		PROPHYLACTIC MEASURES				NONE	1
None	1	Anti-D given	2	Date	Sign.		
Pelvis	2	Rubella vaccine given	3	Date	Sign.		
Other (specify)	3	Other (specify)	4	Date	Sign.		

POST-NATAL NOTES

23/08/02 *Seen post-delivery*

Baby f - externally looks normal c̄ no
dysmorphic features

Consent for full PM obtained

Neither Jennifer or other us to see baby

Wants to go home

Sec b-8/n at present once PM result available

yellow fev

OPERATION(S) in PUERPERIUM				NONE	1	
Uterine evacuation	2	Resuture perineum	3	Hysterectomy		4
Sterilisation	5	Resuture abdomen	6	Other		7
Date		Anaesthetic		Anaesthetist		
Surgeon		Assistant				
Procedure						

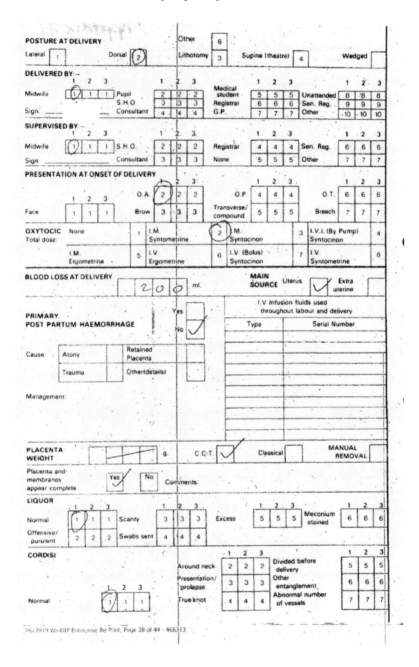

POSTURE AT DELIVERY

Lateral	1	Dorsal	(2)	Other	6				
				Lithotomy	3	Supine (theatre)	4	Wedged	

DELIVERED BY:-

	1	2	3		1	2	3		1	2	3		1	2	3
Midwife	(1)	1	1	Pupil	2	2	2	Medical student	5	5	5	Unattended	8	8	8
				S.H.O.	3	3	3	Registrar	6	6	6	Sen. Reg.	9	9	9
Sign:				Consultant	4	4	4	G.P.	7	7	7	Other	10	10	10

SUPERVISED BY:-

	1	2	3		1	2	3		1	2	3		1	2	3
Midwife	(1)	1	1	S.H.O.	2	2	2	Registrar	4	4	4	Sen. Reg.	6	6	6
Sign:				Consultant	3	3	3	None	5	5	5	Other	7	7	7

PRESENTATION AT ONSET OF DELIVERY

	1	2	3		1	2	3		1	2	3		1	2	3
				O.A.	(2)	2	2	O.P.	4	4	4	O.T.	6	6	6
Face	1	1	1	Brow	3	3	3	Transverse/ compound	5	5	5	Breech	7	7	7

OXYTOCIC Total dose:

None		I.M. Syntometrine	1	M. Syntocinon	(2)	I.V.I. (By Pump) Syntocinon	3		4
I.M. Ergometrine		I.V. Ergometrine	5	I.V. (Bolus) Syntocinon	6	I.V. Syntometrine	7		8

BLOOD LOSS AT DELIVERY 2 0 0 ml.   **MAIN SOURCE** Uterus   Extra uterine ✓

PRIMARY POST PARTUM HAEMORRHAGE   Yes [ ]   No [✓]

I.V infusion fluids used throughout labour and delivery

Type	Serial Number

Cause	Atony	Retained Placenta
	Trauma	Other(details)

Management:

PLACENTA WEIGHT [ ] 9   C.C.T. [✓]   Classical [ ]   **MANUAL REMOVAL** [ ]

Placenta and membranes appear complete   Yes [✓]   No [ ]   Comments:

LIQUOR

	1	2	3		1	2	3		1	2	3		1	2	3
Normal	1	1	1	Scanty	3	3	3	Excess	5	5	5	Meconium stained	6	6	6
Offensive/ purulent	2	2	2	Swabs sent	4	4	4								

CORD(S)

		1	2	3		1	2	3		1	2	3
	Around neck	2	2	2	Divided before delivery	5	5	5				
	Presentation/ prolapse	3	3	3	Other entanglement	6	6	6				
Normal (1) 1 1	True knot	4	4	4	Abnormal number of vessels	7	7	7				

135

SPONTANEOUS / OPERATIVE DELIVERY NOTES (Incl. Perineal Repair)

Date 23/8/02.   Anaesthetic   Anaesthetist

Surgeon   Assistant   Midwife

PROCEDURE

SVD of female baby.
I.M. Syntometrine on delivery
Delivery of placenta by maternal effort & cct.
Perineum intact.

SWABS (PERINEAL REPAIR)

Initial   Final
Count _____   Count _____

Sutures for removal (& number) _____   Signature _____

Weeks   Days   Checked By _____

GESTATION AT DELIVERY (known or best guess)		2	4	5		PLACE OF DELIVERY					
					Clarendon Wing	1	Otley	2	Home	3	
INDICATIONS FOR OPERATIVE DELIVERY						Spontaneous Delivery	1		1	1	
Prolonged labour	2	2	2	Hypertension	12	12	12	To avoid maternal effort / maternal exhaustion	21	21	21
Malposition	3	3	3	Glucose intolerance	13	13	13				
Fetal hypoxia	4	4	4	Iso-Immunisation	14	14	14	Suspect or known Uterine rupture	22	22	22
Scarred uterus	5	5	5	Age	15	15	15				
Prematurity	6	6	6	Placenta praevia	16	16	16	Genital tract malformation	23	23	23
Growth retardation	7	7	7	Other A.P.H.	17	17	17				
Infertility	8	8	8	Cord Accident	18	18	18	Pelvic tumours (cysts, fibroids, etc)	24	24	24
Bad obstetric history	9	9	9	Prolonged 2nd stage	19	19	19				
Breech	10	10	10	Other (Specify)	20	20	20	Fetopelvic disproportion	25	25	25
Multiple Pregnancy	11	11	11								

Department of Feto maternal Medicine
Email:
Contact:
Tel:
Fax:
Our Ref:
Your Ref:
Date: 2 September 2002

Dear

Jennifer ELLIOTT dob

I write with the sad outcome of Jennifer's pregnancy. As you will be aware, in her previous pregnancy we diagnosed that her baby had Dandy Walker malformation and a cardiac defect. In the current pregnancy this baby appears to have a different cardiac defect and a different cranial defect in that is appears to have agenesis of the corpus callosum. After much deliberation she opted for a termination and a very difficult fetocide was performed, following which she was admitted for induction of labour. She subsequently delivered a stillborn female infant of some 700 grams.

I have arranged to see her in the combined obstetric/genetic clinic in six weeks' time when we will discuss the results of the post mortem.

Kind regards.

Yours sincerely

Consultant in Feto maternal Medicine

I felt very isolated in my thoughts after giving birth. I didn't know anyone in the same situation. Surprisingly, ARC, (Antenatal Results and Choices) are now able to estimate from the available statistics that at least five thousand Terminations for Medical Reasons (TFMR) happen in the UK every year. Back then, the number would have been lower because scanning and testing equipment was less advanced and therefore, parent choice and medical advice on whether to terminate was limited compared to today. However, despite better testing being available for my babies, there weren't any support groups available so I didn't have the chance to meet other parents who had gone through the same experience as me, and I felt really alone. I often wonder if social media would have been helpful to me, or too painful to access. Had my experiences happened after the development of social media, I would have been able to reach out for support from relevant Facebook groups and talk to women going through similar experiences. These days people seem to have more interest in understanding medical terms so they can discuss their exact issues with others on social media, including using abbreviated medical terms for simplicity, too. When abbreviations are mentioned in social posts, it automatically informs the reader how they experienced their loss. Support and communication in this area has evolved massively due to social media and when I think of the laborious hours I've spent explaining my experiences over the years, I really wish I'd had this. On the flip side, though, I also wonder whether the glamorization of motherhood that we now endure through celebrity parents via the media would have been too much to bear.

In the week after Jessie's birth, we were inundated with flowers and cards of condolence. It was like a recurring nightmare after what I had been through with Andrew. Mark was grieving. I tried to comfort him, but I felt numb and selfishly told myself that he couldn't be suffering as much I was. Even the thought of registering Jessie's birth, or going to the funeral, was too painful. How could I look at another little white coffin? When we did finally pluck up the courage to register her birth, we arrived at the register office at the same time as a couple who had a new baby with them. They were so happy and excited to be registering the birth of their perfect baby. It was a heart-breaking experience and all we came away with, was Jessie's still birth certificate while the other couple went home with their beautiful baby and everything to look forward to.

The funeral was heart-wrenching. I didn't help with any of the planning. I just couldn't face it. Only Mark and I attended. It was simple and unmemorable. I have certainly locked some memories away deeper than others and have very few memories of the day. Just the unshakable feelings of grief and dread.

Six weeks after I gave birth to Jessie, I had a mental health assessment which concluded that I had recovered remarkably well psychologically. However, in all honesty I don't think I will ever fully recover.

I saw the counsellor from the genetics team once after the birth. They had been unable to find any genetic issues after testing me and were a bit stumped as to what advice to give. They suggested a 1 in 4 chance of recurrence of abnormalities in subsequent pregnancies which was no different than before. I didn't have any therapy and was good at putting on a brave face. I didn't want my family to worry about me. We had made the decision not to carry on with the pregnancy and now I had to face the consequences. I was in a much worse place than I acknowledged, though: Mark took me to Asda one Sunday to pick up something for dessert as we were going to visit his grandad and wanted to take him a treat. I sat in the car crying while Mark went in. I couldn't face going inside and seeing pregnant women and happy families with babies. I was depressed and felt like a total failure.

Department of Feto maternal Medicine
E-mail:
Contact:
Tel:
Fax:
Our Ref:
Your Ref:
Date: 17 October 2002

Dear Dr Bolton

Jennifer ELLIOTT dob

I saw Jennifer and her partner ⎯⎯⎯ today at the Genetics Clinic along with Dr ⎯⎯⎯ Consultant in Clinical Genetics. As you know, Jennifer lost her second baby with abnormalities approximately six weeks ago. She appears to be coping remarkably well from a psychological point of view and has made a good physical recovery. The post mortem results confirm the ante-natally diagnosed agenesis of the corpus callosum along with Fallot's tetralogy. The female fetus was appropriately grown for gestational age. Other features noted at post mortem were bilateral hydronephrosis and severe tongue-tie with virtually absent sublingual frenulum.

Overall the combination of abnormalities do not fit with any particular syndrome. After a long discussion with the geneticists again there does not appear to be any particular link between the abnormalities in this pregnancy and with Jennifer's first pregnancy. Both babies had a cardiac abnormality which, would potentially increase her risk of having another baby with a cardiac abnormality. There does not appear to be any pattern of genetic inheritance to account for the two pregnancy problems that Jennifer has had, however we are left with a situation where it is very difficult to give any definitive recurrence risk for them as a couple. In a subsequent pregnancy we would want to see Jennifer at an early stage to assess viability, and then we would perform a nuchal-translucency scan at around 12 weeks. In view of her increased risk of having a baby with cardiac abnormalities if the nuchal translucency was normal at 12 weeks this would be very reassuring. I have said that we would scan her probably every two weeks in the first and second trimester to assess the anatomy, and hopefully in any subsequent pregnancy this would be normal. Jennifer has had a lot of support from the Genetic Counsellors who will continue to have contact with her.

I have not personally arranged to see her again, but will be happy to do so should she have any further questions. We will be happy to see her in a subsequent pregnancy.

Yours sincerely

Subspecialty Training Fellow in Feto maternal Medicine

We soon had an appointment to discuss the findings of the post-mortem and how we would move forward to get a diagnosis. I felt that there must be something wrong with me. Both babies had such prolific abnormalities yet had different fathers. The problem must be due to me. I asked if my ovaries or eggs could be tested in the hope that they would be able to see if there was anything of concern. However, Lynn

Johnson said that they would have to remove my ovaries in order to test them. Well, that wasn't an option was it?!

The post-mortem showed that Jessie had additional abnormalities. They diagnosed a more serious and rarer syndrome that couldn't even be tested for. I was reassured and strangely relieved to hear this information and knew then that I had made the right decision for Jessie. She would have been very poorly, lived a short life and her quality of life would have been poor. I will always wonder if a miracle could have happened if I had gone through with having Jessie though, and I have often felt suffocated by guilt over the years. I didn't lose my baby. I chose not to have her. I wanted to know that my child wouldn't be in pain and have to endure numerous operations that could in fact lead to losing her anyway. Sometimes I have felt as if the decision punished me more than it did Jessie. I have also often felt that it would have been easier (for me) to have continued with the pregnancy and to have dealt with the consequences later.

You can only judge other people's decisions when you have walked in their shoes. My shoes were extremely painful now. In fact, it felt like there were nine-inch nails stabbing through my feet in every step I took.

FINAL POSTMORTEM EXAMINATION REPORT

PATHOLOGIST		UNIT NO:			
		CONSULTANT:			
St James's University Hospital		SURNAME:	ELLIOTT		
Beckett Street		FIRST NAMES:	Female Fetus of Jennifer		
Leeds		ADDRESS:			
LS9 7TF					
HOSPITAL: LGI	WARD: Delivery Suite	DATE OF DELIVERY: 23.08.02	GESTATION: 24 Weeks		PM NO:
DATE OF PM: 28.08.02		PLACE OF PM: St James's University Hospital			

FINAL ANATOMICAL DIAGNOSIS:
Tetralogy of Fallot
Absent corpus callosum

CLINICAL DETAILS:

The mother is 21 years of age. She has had a previous termination of pregnancy for fetal malformation. This fetus had a Dandy Walker malformation of the brain, a pelvic kidney and polydactyly of the feet. In the current pregnancy the LMP was March 2002 and EDD 08.12.02. An ultrasound scan showed that the fetus had Fallot's tetralogy and an absent corpus callosum. The parents opted for induction of labour. An amniocentesis showed no evidence of deletion of Chromosome 22.

A female fetus was delivered 23.08.02 at 0115hrs.

Written maternal consent was obtained for an unrestricted autopsy examination. The mother consented to the retention of the brain and heart as required and requested that these were cremated in a seemly manner by the pathology laboratory.

EXTERNAL APPEARANCES:

The body is that of a female fetus of body weight and measurements appropriate for the stated gestational age. There is a mild degree of maceration of the skin with extensive discolouration and skin slippage over the extremities. There are no dysmorphic features. The ears are not low set or posteriorly rotated. The eyes are normally positioned. There is no abnormal slanting of the palpebral fissures. The nares are not anteverted and the nasal bridge is not depressed. There is marked tongue-tie with the tip of the tongue firmly tethered by an extremely short frenulum. No antenatal teeth are seen and there are no oral hamartomata. The neck, back, thorax and abdomen are unremarkable on examination. The spinal column is normal to palpation. There are five digits on each extremity. The palmar skin creases are normal. There is no talipes. The external genitalia are those of a normal female fetus and the anus is patent.

ELLIOTT, Female Fetus of Jennifer .
11.09.02

143

Weight:	594g	Head circumference:	21.1cm
Crown-heel length:	30.3cm	Chest circumference:	19.5cm
Crown-rump length:	19.6cm	Abdominal circumference:	16.0cm
Foot length:	4.3cm		

INTERNAL EXAMINATION:

Central Nervous system

The skin of the scalp is rather lax and reflects easily to reveal normally formed cranial bones. The sutures are not fused. The anterior fontanelle is of normal size. The brain weighs 84g which is appropriate for the stated gestation. There are two cerebral hemispheres and an intact interhemispheric fissure. The gyral pattern is appropriate for the gestational age. The brainstem and cerebellum appear unremarkable. No posterior fossa cyst is identified. The aqueduct of Sylvius is identified and is not dilated. The corpus callosum which is usually readily identified at this gestation is not apparent. Following fixation the brain was further examined. The corpus callosum was definitely identified. On sectioning there is no ventricular dilatation and no areas of haemorrhage are seen. The spinal cord has not been formally examined.

Cardiovascular system

The pericardium is intact. There is no pericardial effusion. The heart weighs 3.4g which is towards the lower end of the normal range for this gestation. The heart is in atrial situs solitus and the apex is directed left. The right atrium receives blood from the inferior and superior venae cavae which are unremarkable. The right ventricle is obviously hypertrophied and the pulmonary valve is stenotic. The valve cusps are slightly thickened and probably dysplastic. There is perimembranous ventriculoseptal defect present with overriding of the aorta above this. The left side of the heart is normally formed with no abnormality of the mitral valve. The ductus arteriosus and foramen ovale are patent.

Respiratory system

The trachea and main bronchi are normally formed. There is no tracheo-oesophageal fistula. No diaphragm or webs are identified with the tracheal lumen. The right lung weighs 10.8g and the left lung weighs 10.3g. These weights are appropriate for the gestational age and body weight. The pleural surface of the lungs is entirely smooth with no formation of the pulmonary fissures. The lungs are not hypoplastic. Sections show no focal abnormality. There are no pleural effusions. The diaphragm is intact.

Gastrointestinal system

The mouth is normally formed although there is pronounced tongue-tie as described above. The oesophagus is patent throughout its length. The stomach and duodenum are in situs solitus and the stomach contains a small amount of mucus. The small and large bowel are normally fixed and rotated. No atretic segments are seen. There is meconium is present throughout the length of the bowel.

The liver weighs 21.3g which is appropriate for the body weight and gestational age. The liver is normally formed and no focal lesion is seen on sectioning. The gall bladder is appropriately positioned.

Genito-urinary system

The right kidney weighs 2.8g and the left kidney weighs 3.3g. These weights are appropriate for body weight and gestational age. There is marked bilateral hydronephrosis with dilatation of the renal pelvis and mild thinning of the cortex. No cystic change is seen. The ureters can be traced to the bladder. There is no hydroureter. The bladder is of normal size.

Haemopoietic system

The spleen weighs 0.7g and is normally positioned. The thymus gland weighs 1.5g (appropriate for gestation) and is unremarkable in appearance.

Endocrine system

The right adrenal gland weighs 0.9g and the left adrenal gland weighs 0.8g. These weights are appropriate for body weight and gestational age. The adrenal glands are normally positioned and unremarkable on sectioning. There is no haemorrhage, necrosis or calcification. The pancreas gland is unremarkable. The thyroid gland and pituitary gland are normally formed.

Musculoskeletal system

No fractures are identified and the muscle bulk appears normal.

Placenta

The placenta weighs 212g complete and 168g trimmed. It measures 14 x 14 x 1.5cm and is discoid in shape. The membranes are complete and translucent and the fetal surface is clear. The cord is 20cm in length and contains three vessels. The cord is detached from the placenta and there is a large central defect in the placental parenchyma corresponding to the site of insertion of the cord. Sectioning shows no focal abnormality.

SPECIAL INVESTIGATIONS:

Histology of fetal tissues and placenta.
Karyotyping from skin and placenta.

HISTOLOGY:

Intestine – Two muscle coats are present. Ganglion cells are identified. The mucosa is severely autolysed but appears to be normally formed otherwise.

Thymus – The thymus has a normal lobular pattern. No stress changes are seen.

Adrenal gland – The definitive cortex and fetal cortex are developing normally. There is no calcification and no necrosis is seen. No viral inclusions are present.

Spleen – Appropriate development for gestation.

Lungs – The lungs are in the canalicular stage of development consistent with gestational age. Occasional aspirated squames are present. There is no intrauterine pneumonia. The bronchovascular distribution is normal.

Skeletal muscle – Unremarkable. There is no significant variation in fibre in size.

Pancreas – Severely autolysed. Endocrine and exocrine elements are present.

Neck structures – Normally formed. The tracheal lumen is patent.

Kidneys – The renal parenchyma is severely autolysed but there is severely autolysed but there is ongoing glomerulogenesis. No cystic dysplastic is identified.

Liver – No ductal plate malformation is seen. There is no cystic change within the liver. Extramedullary haemopoesis is abundant.

Placenta – There is no inflammation of the extraplacental membranes. Three vessels are seen within the umbilical cord. The chorionic villi are large and immature consistent with the gestational age. There is no villitis or intervillositis. No areas of infarction are seen. There is no maternal vasculopathy.

Heart – There is autolysis of the cardiac muscle fibres with disintegration of the tissue. No fibrosis is seen and there is no calcification. No endocardial fibroelastosis is present.

Brain – Despite fixation there is some fragmentation of the cerebral tissue, however, the cortex is laminar and neuronal migration appears to be progressing normally. There is no dysplasia of the olivary nuclei and the basal ganglia are normally formed. There is no obvious dilatation of the lateral ventricles and no haemorrhage or ischaemic change is seen.

SUMMARY OF FINDINGS:

1. Mildly macerated female fetus of appropriate size for gestational age.

2. Severe tongue-tie with virtually absent sublingual frenulum.

3. Fallot's tetralogy of heart.

4. Bilateral hydronephrosis.

5. Absent pulmonary fissures.

6. Absent corpus callosum.

ELLIOTT, Female Fetus of Jennifer
11-09-02   4

COMMENT:

The autopsy examination of this female fetus confirms the antenatal diagnosis of Fallot's tetralogy and absent corpus callosum. Other minor anomalies are identified and in view of the previously affected fetus of this patient genetic advice is recommended.

Note that the brain and heart were retained for fixation in accordance with parental consent. After examination these organs will be respectfully dealt with by the pathology laboratory.

Consultant Paediatric Pathologist

We collected Jessie's ashes and again in a very low-key event scattered them with her brother's ashes at the top of mum and dad's garden. We bought another tree to go with Andrew's, which was now well established and had strong branches. He would protect his little sister Jessie, and their deep roots would be entwined for years to come.

Chapter 8: Dark times

Six weeks after I'd given birth to Jessie, Mark and I went on holiday to Kos in Greece with Katie and Steven. Diane and Ty had also planned to accompany us but the week before, Ty was involved in an unprovoked attack on his way home from work in Leeds city centre and got stabbed in the chest. It was a nasty injury. I visited him in hospital soon after and the doctor I saw doing his rounds told me that he was lucky to be alive! We felt awful going away without them but Ty was recovering well and insisted we go.

The holiday was as enjoyable as it could be under the circumstances. I was still bleeding and my body felt big and squishy. We drank lots of alcohol and relaxed in the sun and I almost felt like I could face the world again. I had finished university that summer and attained a higher-level diploma. I was now a qualified youth worker and would be paid more money per hour than ever for working in a job I loved and I was also looking for another job to go alongside. I had left the school I was working at when I began my youth work job, as going to college to study a full-time course had been more than enough to keep me busy. If I had been provided with the correct information from either hospital, midwife or even college, I would have discovered that I was entitled to take full maternity leave due to my still birth happening after twenty-four weeks. I am not sure I would have taken maternity leave anyway, as I had found that keeping busy helped to keep my mind occupied and my thoughts away from Jessie.

As Mark had lived in his council flat for such a long time, we could get a good discount if we bought it, so we were thinking about that. We were also talking about getting engaged. I really wanted to get engaged, which I admit translated to:" I want a big sparkly ring and a party". I needed something to look forward to and this was the perfect idea. Despite the fact that he was usually quite strong willed and would have relished being in charge of our major life decisions, I think Mark now felt so sorry for me and he would just let me have my way. I wanted to try again straight away for another baby but Mark wanted me to concentrate on getting a job and buying the flat. Perhaps he thought that the promise of us getting engaged would pacify me and take my mind off trying again. We loved each other and had been through so much together, but I was struggling to talk to Mark about how I was coping and once again I just didn't feel that we were on the same page in terms of our plans for the future. It would have been sensible to wait because my body had been through so much and probably needed a break from pregnancy, but again the pull of my maternal need for a baby was so strong. I was like an addict that could never escape the hunger for a baby in order to feel complete.

A job working for The Children's Society charity came up and I applied and got the position of Advocacy Support Worker. The position was eighteen hours a week, which balanced well with my eighteen hours working for the Youth Service. The main purpose of the post was to support the police when a young person went missing. If a child between the ages of twelve and sixteen went missing and then returned home, we would receive a report about the case and organise a home visit. We would usually then refer the family to another agency, or if we had capacity to, we would work with the young person for a period of about eight weeks to resolve any issues they had at home or school. I was twenty-two now and really enjoyed my work. I it opened my eyes to the diverse ways in which people lived and I found it both satisfying and interesting. Visiting houses in deprived areas of Leeds and dealing with families with complex needs made me appreciate my life and the opportunities I had. Giving birth to Andrew at the age of seventeen was traumatic and life changing but I had support from my family, a roof over my head and financial help. The realisation that some people didn't have the support and guidance that I was lucky enough to have was humbling for me. I have always had natural empathy for others and this important skill came into its' own in my new role.

Mark and I got engaged that summer. He proposed to me in lovely restaurant on Call Lane in Leeds. He didn't get down on one knee and the proposal was rather contrived as I knew about the ring, but he still made it romantic. My mum's neighbour owned a jewellery business and designed and made a stunning single solitaire ring with a heart shaped setting in white gold for us. It was beautiful and I was so excited to wear it. After the meal we went for drinks in a livelier part of town. I overdid things somewhat and threw up mushroom risotto all over our bed when I got home. Mark said to my mum the next day. "Take her out for a posh meal and she hacks it all back up over the bed when we get home". Oh dear… not a good start to the engagement! He soon forgave me and we started to plan the engagement party, which was to take place at a local health club and hotel. We invited all our friends and family and now had something wonderful to look forward to. We decorated the venue with pink balloons and decorations and I asked everyone to wear pink. It was really special and my sisters and I danced all night.

Soon after the engagement party, I thought I was pregnant again. It had been around eight months since we'd lost Jessie and I was apprehensive but didn't want to give up on my dream and was in a good place to try again. I hoped that as soon as we purchased the flat, we could sell it and buy a little house with a garden. I bought a test and Katie stayed with me while I did it. Despite the result being quite faint…it was positive! Mark was quiet and moody about it at first. He wanted a bit more time to sort out our finances and buy the flat before thinking about having another baby. He had also become quite distant and was spending lots of time out drinking with his friends. I hadn't lost much baby weight from being pregnant with Jessie and I looked pale and tired. Now, pregnant again, I felt frumpy, fat and ugly and it didn't help that Mark never complimented on my appearance in either a positive or negative way. I was nervous about the pregnancy and I couldn't talk to Mark. I also didn't want to tell anyone in my family or any of my friends that I was pregnant. I couldn't face their anguish and worry as well as my own.

The nine-week scan soon came and I walked into the Clarendon Wing feeling great, though slightly anxious to be back at this familiar haunt. I should probably have been worried about the lack of pregnancy symptoms I had been experiencing, but I'd told myself that perhaps that fact that I didn't feel sick and poorly meant that my baby was healthy. Lynn Johnson welcomed us with open arms and was pleased to hear our news. When she scanned me, she could see the sac but couldn't find a heartbeat. She reassured us that maybe my dates were a little behind and they would be able to see more at twelve weeks.

The twelve-week scan never came.

At ten weeks I started to bleed and was in extreme pain. I had an emergency scan where they could see a sac but again couldn't find a heartbeat. They were still hopeful at this point that that there was a chance that the pregnancy could progress normally. I hadn't had an early miscarriage before and didn't think I ever would. Doctors had always told me that my poorly babies should naturally have miscarried due to their abnormalities but also that my body had clung on to them because I was young and healthy.

I woke up late on the Saturday night in absolute agony. You could barely see the sheets for blood and as I stood up, I lost a massive clot the size of a large orange. Mark wrapped and covered me with bath towels to soak up the blood and rushed me to A&E. I didn't even bother to change my pyjama bottoms because they were saturated. As soon as we arrived, I was taken to a ward to be kept under observation.

Mark went home because he had work in the morning. (He later told me that he couldn't face being with me through the miscarriage and was finding our relationship stressful. He even told me that he wasn't sure that he still loved me at this point.).

Katie was at my bedside the next morning. It had been a horrible night. I had bled so much that they'd had to remove some large clots to stop the bleeding. I was told that I would need a D&C procedure that day to remove retained parts of the pregnancy sac. Katie tried to comfort me as best she could and I was so glad to see her friendly face. Looking back, I don't believe that this pregnancy was ever anything more than the growing gestational sac, as my symptoms had been so vague and felt minor compared to previous pregnancies.

My sisters came to see me that day. Susie was very upset and couldn't believe this had happened again. I tried to comfort her and stay optimistic. I was utterly bereft but even that day, I knew I would not give up on my dream: I was determined to have a healthy baby. I had the D&C procedure that afternoon and my dad later drove me back home to Mark who had been working overtime all day. There was a distance between us that night. The grief was unbearable and I sat once again and cried the night away.

After the miscarriage, Mark and I soon began to drift apart and our relationship deteriorated massively. We both started going out separately on nights out and spent time with our friends, rather than each other. I lost a lot of weight and was feeling good about my appearance and as a result, I received plenty of male attention on nights out. I was no angel and was flirting with different lads on nights out. I think I was rebelling as all I wanted to do was to go out, get drunk and escape from myself. But going out was a temporary fix and I often ended up hungover and depressed. I would have swapped that life in a heartbeat to be at home in my PJ's with a couple of screaming babies and a cup of tea.

My periods were all over the place and Mark and I were barely having sex. After the miscarriage, we had been to the hospital where the experts looked at each of our medical histories. They had offered us help and support to get pregnant by using a procedure called Ovulation Induction. This is where fertility drugs are used to monitor and induce ovulation. Couples are then advised of the specific dates to have sex in order to conceive. It isn't as invasive as IVF but it still involves being monitored regularly. It's ideal for women with irregular periods who are struggling to conceive. I had already been diagnosed with polycystic ovaries, which is a hormonal condition that can affect your ability to conceive naturally, so I was an ideal candidate.

Mark jumped into the conversation and said we were going to have a break from trying to conceive. He had clearly made this decision alone! I was so angry with him for doing this and told him that I wanted to accept the offer of fertility treatment because I felt that they would really support us and give us a good chance of having a healthy baby.

The next day, I called the clinic back to accept the offer of treatment, assuming it was still available. Mark was none the wiser that I had made this phone call. I told him that I couldn't stay with him if he wasn't with me on this and he reluctantly agreed to come back to the fertility clinic. Whilst we waited for this appointment to come through, things were actually going from bad to worse in our relationship. Mark went out one night and came back at around seven in the morning. His car windscreen had been smashed and as I cleaned up the glass inside the car, I found a note on the seat. It said: "I know it was you". Social Media didn't exist yet, so of course sending messages and shaming people online for all to see wasn't possible back then. I didn't have to be Miss Marple to work out that he had upset someone's boyfriend! Boy code was strong in his circle and I wasn't able to find out the truth.

The final straw for me was when Mark made me spaghetti Bolognese with meat, when I had been a vegetarian for three years! I'd had enough and decided to move back to my mum's. How I held down my full-time job at this time in my life, I don't know. My mental health was terrible but I just couldn't articulate how I felt and really didn't want to try. Mark sent me a rose every day for a week after I left him and sent me a card, saying that he would only stop loving me when they found a tear in the ocean. It made me realise that he did care about me and was trying to make things right between us, but at the time I thought it was too little too late.

I made things far worse by having a fling with another lad from Horsforth, Aidan, who was in the same friendship group as Mark. He also had a bad relationship with his mum and was very needy. Was there a pattern forming? Was I trying to play a motherly role for these men?

Shortly after he found out about the fling, Mark invited his ex-girlfriend from years ago back to our flat overnight. He claimed nothing happened and apparently, she had laid on the bed naked, and he still turned her down. Could I really believe this story? We were hurting each other and our families. Katie and I weren't speaking much and had fallen out over what was happening. She'd heard rumours that I had been sleeping with another man and obviously was going to take her brother's side. Mark made everything worse for me by storming around to my mum and dad's house shouting about what a 'bitch' I had been. I was now in self-destruct mode!

Mark and I continued to ring each other and saw each other all the time. We had a strong bond despite the hurt and pain we had caused each other. I was so insecure on my own and needed Mark around. I felt he was the only person who understood what I had been through. So, when we eventually got the letter through from the fertility clinic a few months later, we decided to make a fresh start of our relationship. In hindsight, we should probably not have got back together, but my desire to be pregnant again was so strong that I was clinging on to the hope that I could be happy and have a baby with Mark.

We started the treatment in September 2004. Mark was asked to give a sperm sample and I had a scan. I was sent away with a supply of Clomid tablets, which I was told would help me to ovulate. They would then scan me during the next month to see if we had been successful. We were still all over the place in trying to restore our relationship and we were now also isolated from friends and family. Everyone, including my parents, thought we were crazy to have got back together after all the fall outs and infidelity. How could we build trust and get our once loving relationship back on track?

A holiday of a lifetime, perhaps?

Chapter 9: Maldives

In early December 2004 I had been taking Clomid for two months and not yet fallen pregnant. I went to all the appointments by myself because Mark was ambivalent about us trying for a baby in this way. We decided it would be good for us to get away and go on a romantic holiday to escape the hell at home. I was still getting hassle from the lad I had been seeing whilst Mark and I had briefly separated and I couldn't face Christmas and New Year with our families. I just wanted to get away.

We maxed out our credit cards and booked a two-week trip to the Maldives. The photographs in the brochure made the islands look like paradise and this was somewhere I had only dreamed of going before. The furthest I'd travelled so far was to Spain and Greece. This would be the trip that would save our relationship.

A week or so before we left, one of my mum's friends helped me to book the holiday on the Internet. We would travel independently and arrange accommodation and travel options ourselves. We were due to leave on the 22nd of December and would arrive home on 3rd January. We were so excited and I was thrilled that we could leave all the crap at home and enjoy Christmas together in the sun. We had been through hell during the past couple of years and we deserved this. I told the clinicians at the hospital about the holiday and they commented that it would be amazing to conceive in Paradise. It would be a dream come true.

So, we set off on our adventure from Manchester airport, apprehensive but buzzing with adrenaline for our holiday. We would be staying on a small island for much of the trip and then go to a larger, more luxurious island for New Year. We landed in the capital city of Mali and took a speed boat to the tiny island. The journey was the experience of a lifetime and my heart was in my mouth as we bounced on the waves. I was overwhelmed by the beauty and simplicity of the surroundings. The staff were welcoming and we were shown to a simple yet picturesque room. The island was extremely small and primitive. There were only about twenty-five guests and maybe ten members of staff on the whole island. The beaches were stunning with clear water and an abundance of sea life. It took eight minutes to walk around the island and small reef sharks swam close to the edge of the beach. The only restaurant was small and simply set out and the bar was in a beautiful wooden gazebo, surrounded by crystal-clear sea water. It was so peaceful and relaxing and for the first few days it was amazing. I remember wishing that I had taken more books with me to fill the time. Mark wasn't a big reader and I read Paul Gascoigne's autobiography out loud to him whilst laid on the beach. Breakfast, lunch and tea consisted of Sri Lankan curry dishes. Many of the staff on the island were Sri Lankan. It is common for them to work in the tourist parts of the Maldives for part of the year and then travel home to their families for the rest of the year with the money they've earned to support them. I ate a lot of bread on this holiday. The food was tasty but I really didn't fancy curry for breakfast! We spent Christmas Day on the beach enjoying a small celebration with a variety of delicious food. Unfortunately, we hadn't made many friends as most of the other guests were Japanese, so the language barrier was tricky. We met a friendly couple from the Netherlands and got to know them quite well but it was a bit lonely at times and I felt this especially on Christmas Day.

On Boxing Day, I was sat alone reading on the beach when there was suddenly a big commotion and everyone was ushered quickly to our rooms. We didn't understand what was happening but there was a strange feeling in the air and the sea looked unsettled. I didn't panic too much because I initially thought it might be a regular occurrence. When we went down for lunch though, there was a worrying atmosphere and I sensed a feeling of concern amongst the staff. We spoke to our friends from the Netherlands who explained that there had been an earthquake in Sri Lanka and several family members of the staff on the island had died. We didn't understand the magnitude of the situation at this point and were completely unaware that there had been a catastrophic tsunami killing thousands of people.

That evening, all guests on the island received a typed letter informing us there had been a tsunami, but of course we were still unaware of the of impact of this on the rest on the world and were oblivious to the fact that the news from our tiny island was also global news. We didn't have a working mobile phone or even a television to watch. We were obviously very concerned for the staff and uneasy about the upset and unrest on our island. The next day, another typed letter arrived, telling us that some families had been rescued from nearby islands and would be arriving on our island that day. These people had lost all of their belongings, so we were asked to donate any spare clothes or toiletries. The letter also told us to prepare for aftershocks from the earthquake and to be on alert. This was all becoming quite alarming. The couple from the Netherlands contacted home and advised us to do the same as our families would be worried. I eventually managed to get through to my mum and dad on the landline phone at reception. They answered anxiously and immediately burst into floods of tears. I had never heard my dad so distraught. They had been so worried that our island had been washed away like hundreds of others had in the Maldives. My mum and dad unravelled all of the devastating details to me as my jaw hit the floor. I was speechless and in shock and just couldn't believe what had happened. I suddenly felt very vulnerable and wanted to be at home but knew there was no way that this was going to happen anytime soon. I picked up a gin and tonic at the bar and went back to the beach to count our blessings and sunbathe in the warm sunshine.

We spent the last few days of the holiday on a larger, more commercial island. It reminded me of Centre Parcs but in a much more beautiful setting. You could hire bikes and trek around the perimeter of the island on concrete paths. When we arrived there, many of the British tourists had already been taken home by their tour operators, but as we were travelling independently, we were allowed to stay. Despite the sombre atmosphere, our arrival by sea plane was a fantastic experience. I felt like we were celebrities arriving for our next red-carpet experience. The island was just stunning and so romantic. To be honest, you could be there with a total stranger and you would fall in love in such paradise. But despite the beauty surrounding us, we were now prohibited from swimming in the sea due to the possibility of catching Dysentery and I was scared to even look in the water in case I saw a floating limb. New Year's Eve was sad and reflective. People could sense the grief and also the fear that the tsunami had brought to such a beautiful place. The staff tried hard to make the celebrations special and I haven't to this day ever seen a buffet as colourful and ornate! The things you can carve a carrot and cucumber into to is amazing! It looked too good to eat!

We flew back to a cold, wet and miserable Manchester airport to a surprise greeting from the police and my mum and dad. The police were checking who was arriving back into the U.K as so many people were still reported missing. My mum and dad grabbed hold of us and squeezed me tightly. My mum told me that her friend Cathy, who had helped me to book the trip had said on Boxing Day that if I had died, at least it happened in Paradise. I thought this sounded a bit dramatic, though when we listened to the news and read our mobile phone messages, we realised that it really wasn't.

We were back to reality! I was completely broke, I wasn't pregnant, and I still had complete doubts over my feelings for Mark. But at least I survived the tsunami. I admit now though that at the time I wasn't sure how grateful I was for this!

Part 2

My journey back to you.

Chapter 10: Kian

It shouldn't have been a shock when I found out that I was pregnant again, as it was all I thought about in the months after we returned from the Maldives. I was still taking Clomid to help me to ovulate and although the hospital staff was none the wiser, I had split up with Mark again. Remember the guy I had a fling with when Mark and I split up? Well, he was the father of this baby. Aidan and I weren't a couple when I found out that I was pregnant. I had been flitting between Mark and him since we got back from holiday. I wasn't sleeping with Mark, though. We were arguing constantly and trying to resolve practical issues but I just couldn't end things between us completely. Even when he found out that I was pregnant, we still saw each other for a few weeks on and off but it just led to more hurt for us both and Mark eventually changed his phone number. I didn't hear anything from him for a long time after this.

I had purposefully fallen pregnant with a guy that I didn't really love and doubted I would have any kind of future with. My mind was seriously messed up but nothing would get in the way of me having a baby. The addiction was in full swing. I had timed the sex perfectly and the deed was done. It wasn't very romantic and all I could think during the sex was 'please let this be the time!'.

After an anxious two-week wait, I bought a test at Asda and discovered I was pregnant for the fifth time! When I told Aidan about the pregnancy, he was thrilled at the prospect of becoming a dad. His family were dysfunctional and he clung on to the prospect of being involved in my stable family life. I was already thinking about the long and scary road ahead but he was interested in the pregnancy from day one, and his optimism gave me hope. We decided to give things another chance and I was happy to do this at the time, as it seemed to be my only option. Unfortunately, there was very little trust in our relationship from day one, though. I had gone backwards and forwards to Mark and I knew deep down that this was never going to work. Nevertheless, his support would be welcome and it was good to know that my baby's dad would be there for me. He clearly loved me and proposed soon after we got together.

My parents were now at their wits end with me. I was twenty-four and was still causing them stress and upset. My mum took herself off to bed when she found out that I was pregnant again. I can see now that she must have been out of her mind with worry and scared for my future. Of course, I was also concerned about the future but felt very positive about the fact that I could actually still get pregnant, as I had begun to worry that there must be something wrong with my ovaries or womb. I was also trying to make this a positive experience for Aidan, as this was his first time.

Throughout the pregnancy, I saw my previous consultant Lynn Johnson every two weeks for reassurance. It was a wonderful feeling when all of the tests and scans I underwent looked normal and healthy, each time. Going every two weeks made the pregnancy pass quicker and the constant comfort and care I received from the pregnancy assessment unit was phenomenal. The heartache I went through every time I went to the Clarendon Wing was debilitating, though, as I struggled with memories and flashbacks from my pregnancies with Andrew and Jessie, which were especially strong when I was there. Negative thoughts were constantly popping into my head and horrific memories were at the forefront of my mind as if they had happened yesterday.

At our eighteen-week scan, we found out that we were having a boy. We named him Kian from then on, although I still didn't believe that I would ever hold this baby. Aidan wanted an Irish name and it just stuck. It would have been lovely to have excitedly announced to my mum and dad that we were having a boy, but it was just impossible for any of us to get excited. We moved in with my parents and put our names down for a council house. We didn't expect much of a wait, given that I was pregnant. It was a lot was easier to get housed fifteen years ago than it is now.

My labour started on 7th February. I had been told to go to the hospital as early in labour as I wanted to, due to my history and anxiety over the birth. During a routine visit to our local doctors' surgery at 1.00pm, the midwife told me that I could be in slow labour for days, as my cervix was only one centimetre dilated at this point. The pain was already horrendous. Aidan made it back home from work at 2.30ish. I had been crying down the phone to him in agony and as soon as he arrived, we frantically we made our way to the Clarendon Wing, which was around twenty mins away from home. My waters broke in the car and gushed all over my seat and already I felt the urge to push. By the time we reached the labour ward, I was begging for drugs and throwing up bright orange juice, it's all I had drunk all morning. I was delirious with pain. After the horrendous experiences of birth I had encountered in my life so far, I found it hard to imagine the birth of a healthy baby at the end of this pregnancy and hadn't been able to prepare for how I would feel. After an hour of pushing and less drugs than I would take for a headache, Kian was born at 4.10pm. He arrived on his due date of the 7th February 2006. A healthy boy weighing 8lb 6oz.

I'd done it!!! I finally had a tiny baby of my own in my arms.

A flood of emotions surged through my body and the pain disappeared quickly. Kian latched on to my breast immediately, it was amazing.

We had planned for my mum to be my birth partner. My relationship with Aidan had been very on-and-off throughout the pregnancy and I really wanted her there. She thought I was being dramatic though, and didn't believe I was in full labour, so didn't leave work on time. I told her that morning that I had pains and she said "Just because it's your due date, Jennifer, you don't just wake up in labour!" And off she went to work. I was so relieved to see her and my sisters when they arrived at the hospital; shocked and flustered at the news of Kian's quick arrival.

My mum asked me a question as I held Kian. "How do you feel now that you have everything you have ever wanted?" It was a question that stays with me even now because as I laid there, I knew I had everything I'd ever wanted right there in my arms, but somehow, I didn't feel how I thought I would.

The porter came to move us to the ward from the delivery suite and as I sat in the wheelchair ready to take hold of my baby again, he handed me my medical notes to place on my knee first, then Kian on top of them. I carried my notes containing the pictures of my two still born babies. I still hadn't even seen Jessie! It was a strange, surreal feeling. I was ecstatic to eventually have Kian in my arms, but I felt sad for what I had been through and the guilt of the decisions I'd made seemed worse now, somehow. I was holding my precious baby and I knew now what a mother's love was. How could I have not seen or held Jessie? How could I have made the choice to terminate my babies? This felt like a new burden to carry. But I would bury that burden deep in the back of my mind. My mum's question repeated in my head again and again for years to come and I talked myself into believing that I must be happy now because I had everything I'd ever wanted.

Chapter 11: Beginnings and endings

Someone who has been extremely important and significant in my life over the past fifteen years is my best friend Fiona. We have been on a journey together and our bond is very strong. I met Fiona at the side of a football pitch whilst Aidan and her boyfriend were playing in a match. Aidan had started to make a few friends near to where my mum and dad lived in Farsley. He was good at pool and enjoyed football and socialising, so had joined both football teams at our local pub. He told me that a lad he had met there had a girlfriend who was due a baby around the same time as me. I was about 10 weeks pregnant with Kian at this point and thought it would be brilliant to meet someone who I could share experiences of pregnancy with.

Fiona was twenty at the time and lived locally in a flat with her friends but was planning to move back in with her mum to save money, so that she and her boyfriend Pete would be able to buy their own house. Fiona and I instantly became friends, and we would often text each other about our ongoing pregnancies and any issues we were facing. Our babies were due on the same date, although after our subsequent scans, my due date was changed from the 9th to the 7th of February and Fiona's to the 10th.

I had spoken to Fiona briefly about my past pregnancies quite early on in our friendship, as I was having extra scans under the consultant every two weeks and had other appointments which were in addition to those that Fiona would experience. I had felt the need to explain why because we became close very quickly. It was quite difficult for me to relate to Fiona sometimes because this was her first pregnancy and my fifth, but I was ever the optimist, and Fiona helped me to see having this baby as a fresh start.

We attended antenatal classes together for six weeks leading up to our babies' births. Every week, someone else seemed to give birth and was no longer at class. It was frustrating and we started to feel like we would soon be the only ones left. It was an exciting and daunting time for us both in our own personal ways. Towards the end of our pregnancies we went out for a curry together to try to 'bring the babies along' with spicy food and everyone stared at us with our big pregnant bellies. As you know, I gave birth on the 7th of February. Fiona's baby, Grace was born a few days later on the 13th February. It seemed like a long time between the births at the time, especially as Fiona and her boyfriend Pete had not found out the sex of their baby. It was a lovely surprise when I heard that Kian would now have a little girlfriend. Fiona and I spent lot of time together during maternity leave and relied on each other a lot for support during the first couple of months. Unfortunately, Fiona experienced a long and very traumatic birth and suffered with severe anxiety after her gorgeous Grace was born, so I was glad to be there for her. We would often go to a playgroup or a play gym together and then go shopping or for lunch. I loved our trips out together. People would ask if Kian and Grace were twins. They were a gorgeous pair and both had chubby little faces.

When Kian was two months old, Aidan and I moved into a council house. It was a terraced house on a quiet street in Bramley, which was around ten minutes' drive away from my mum's. The rumour we heard was that the woman who had lived there previously had stabbed her partner and was then evicted, though, which gave me the creeps. The walls in the house were painted bright green and orange, which was not to our taste. It was in a pretty terrible state, so we worked hard to renovate it to a liveable home. We had painted and carpeted the whole house and it was now clean and fresh. Then, when Kian was four months old, I went back to work for the Youth Service two nights a week and life became exhausting. Aidan was in and out of employment, which didn't help. He had worked at the Britvic drinks factory before Kian was born but didn't like the job and left without another job to go to. He eventually settled into working as an electrician's mate. He really enjoyed it and this opportunity led him to qualify as an electrician (he now has his own successful business).

It was a shame that the honeymoon period between us had now worn off and our relationship was in tatters after all the work we had put in to get the house looking so lovely for Kian. I cried on Fiona's and my friend Diane's shoulders many a time. There was no trust in our relationship, and even though it was now the last thing on my mind, he was accusing me of cheating and was constantly checking my phone. Things needed to change because we were both so unhappy and making each other's lives miserable. The arguments were horrendous and I cried to the health visitor about how unhappy I was.

Thankfully, she came to visit me more regularly because of this and was a good support.

The final straw snapped one night when the arguing had escalated. We had both been drinking and it got physical between us. I was seething and could feel my anger raging inside me. I grabbed the nearest weapon, which was a metal corkscrew and hit Aidan around the head with it. Blood instantly poured down his face, and he ran upstairs. Panicking, I phoned the police. He phoned the police. We were both arrested and cautioned for assault. Something that would stay on my record for ten years and would need to be explained whenever I needed a DBS check when applying for a job. It was the end of the line for us as a couple and I never went back after that night. At no time had I ever acted like that before (or since) and it really scared me that I could act that way.

Kian and I moved back in with my mum and dad and were welcomed with open arms. They were thrilled to have us there. Aidan didn't have a close family member who he could move in with, but I knew that Kian would be safe when he stayed overnight with his dad, which he did most weekends after this incident. Aidan was a very passionate parent and has continued to be so, in positive and negative ways throughout Kian's childhood. I could never say that he was a 'bad' dad because he has always tried his best for him in the way he thinks is right. We are all shaped by our upbringings and our beliefs are not always going to be the same as each other's. Kian is very close to his dad and now that he is fifteen, they are more like best pals than father and son. I will always be grateful to him for giving me Kian and I regret some of my behaviour during our relationship, which I am sure he does too. At the end of the day, I used him to have a baby with and then tried to make things work when I knew deep down that we weren't supposed to be together. No doubt he would agree that Kian is the best thing that ever happened to us and would never regret us having him for a second. Kian is a very clever and well-adjusted boy and has always accepted that his parents would never be a couple. He laughs and says he can never imagine us being together romantically.

Research that has been conducted about stress and pregnancy, claims that if you produce a large amount of the stress hormone Cortisol whilst you are pregnant, it can have a detrimental effect on your growing baby and can lead to premature birth or even affect the future emotional development of the child. I was extremely stressed during my pregnancy and was constantly backwards and forwards to my mum's after arguments with Aidan. I had not been an angel before I fell pregnant but had just wanted us to settle down. Unfortunately, Aidan has always loved socialising and having a drink and this didn't stop whilst I was pregnant. I am lucky however that Kian has no lasting effects of the stressful start he had in life and hopefully I got out of a relationship involving interpersonal violence before it affected Kian's emotional wellbeing.

It was now about time for a fresh start and new beginnings for me and my eight-month-old baby. It was good being back at my mum's and I felt settled again. Kian was a little blessing for all of my family. My dad especially adored him and it was wonderful to see their lovely bond grow. I was finally content at home with my family and my beautiful baby.

Chapter 12: Ryan and Zac

I decided to go back to Bradford College to complete my final degree year whilst I was living at my mum and dad's. Now I was a single mum, I could get help to pay for childcare and so Kian went to a little nursery attached to the college for two days a week that I was on campus. I still worked two evenings and one afternoon at the local youth club. This was only for twelve hours per week though, and I needed to work at least sixteen hours to be able to claim Child Tax Credit. A friend of the family managed a local pub called The New Inn and they needed bar staff, so I started working there on a Tuesday lunchtime and Saturday night, which bumped up my hours and allowed me to claim this benefit. Tuesday lunch time wasn't great, it was full of 'oldies' who smoked cigarettes and complained a lot. The area where they sat was known as 'death row' and occasionally one would 'drop off' and there would be an empty seat. However, Saturday night was a laugh. I enjoyed being out of the house and having a break to socialise as well as getting paid for it! We could have a couple of drinks whilst we worked and I got on well with the other bar staff.

It was at The New Inn that I got to know my now husband, Ryan. I had met him before at football when Aidan played for the team. Ryan didn't play but used to heckle on the side-line, usually hungover from the Saturday night. He was loud and very confident when he had a few drinks inside him but when he was sober, he was shy and unassuming. I liked that. Plenty of men would approach me who clearly loved themselves and thought I would fall at their feet. Ryan was different. I knew Ryan's sister quite well, as she and my sister were good friends and we had all been out for drinks together before. Farsley is quite a small place and my sisters and their partners all live near each other, so we share lots of the same friends. Ryan was a very good friend of Pete's, Fiona's boyfriend. The more I got to know him, the more I liked him. He was a mature twenty-three-year-old and seemed ready to settle down. He had a stable job working for Royal Mail as a postman and he owned his own house.

Ryan and I started seeing each other in the November. Our relationship moved quickly and I knew that things were falling into place for me at last. Ryan understood that Kian and I were a package and he accepted and embraced this. I loved how close he became to Kian within such a short space of time. We went on double dates with Pete and Fiona and spent Christmas together with our families. It was the perfect time to get to know each other's traditions and family values. We discovered that we'd had very similar upbringings and that both sets of parents got together in the same year. (They are celebrating their 40th wedding anniversaries this year!). Ryan is very close to his family and especially to his mum. It's important to me that men have respect for their mums and with neither Mark or Aidan having good relationships with their mums, seeing Ryan getting on so well with his mum was a refreshing change. Ryan's family were welcoming and friendly and treated baby Kian as their own grandson from day one. Ryan's dad would crawl around with him on the floor and make him scream with laughter.

Our love grew stronger and after a couple of months we decided to get married. Having both been engaged before, we decided to book the wedding straight away because it just felt so right. My little Kian and I moved into Ryan's house and I felt extremely happy and content. I think my mum and dad were apprehensive about us getting close so quickly at first, but they loved Ryan and his positive family values. They could also see that I had changed for the better. Ryan and I enjoyed staying in as a family at the weekends and we talked a lot about our future as husband and wife. We booked the wedding for the 26th of July the following year, so that we would have over a year to plan and organise everything. Mum, my sisters and I went wedding dress shopping almost straight away and I loved every minute of planning our wedding. I couldn't wait to marry Ryan in the local church where I had been baptized and had taken my first Holy Communion. I had been engaged twice before but never had I felt this passionately about getting married.

After we moved in together, I excitedly began converting the house from a man cave to a cosy family home. Ryan knew straight away that I wanted a baby with him, or rather, lots of babies with him! I told him about how I'd lost two babies late in pregnancy and had miscarriages and fertility problems. Ryan was understanding and surprisingly, he didn't run a mile.

My periods had been so heavy, painful and irregular that I couldn't see me getting pregnant without the Clomid tablets that I had taken before Kian. Again, my maternal pull was as strong as ever. In October, when we had been together just short of a year, we went to see Ryan's grandma, 'Grammy' in hospital. She was poorly nearly the whole time that I knew her but despite being ill, she was the bravest, strongest and most inspirational woman I have ever met. I admired her so much and she always showed so much strength and love, no matter how ill she was feeling. She loved Kian and we tried to visit her most weeks. She'd had a very full life and spoke such words of wisdom, with so many stories to tell. I could have listened to her all day.

On that particular hospital visit, I felt very thirsty. My period was late and had been getting terrible period cramps. I went to the toilet due to feeling a wet sensation which I assumed was my period starting. It was white discharge. Given my past experiences, I had an inkling of what this could be and decided that I would buy a pregnancy test the next day if my period still hadn't come. I arranged to meet Fiona with Grace at Jackaboo's, a local play gym, the next morning. With still no period in sight, I bought a pregnancy test on the way. I quickly sneaked off and did the test in the toilet. It came up positive almost instantly! It was a surreal moment. I was thrilled and couldn't wait to tell Ryan the news. The usual pangs of anxiety and apprehension were there but I was so happy that I had managed to conceive naturally. When I told Ryan later at home his little face went red and I will never forget his smile. He picked me and Kian up in his big six-foot five frame and I felt so safe and loved. I knew that things would always be good in my life now that I had Ryan by my side.

Going to the doctors did upset the apple cart slightly. With my periods being so sporadic, it was difficult to work out my dates. The

175

doctor worked out that my due date would be the 26th of July. It couldn't be! This was to be my wedding day! How could I have a baby then? After some long discussions we decided to bring the wedding forward to March. I would be twenty-five weeks pregnant then, all being well, and fingers crossed I would still fit into the beautiful fishtail silk satin dress that I'd just had altered to fit my slim figure.

The pregnancy progressed successfully and I turned up to my first appointment with Lynn Johnson with dad number four in tow! I felt a little self-conscious and wondered what she must think of me. I am a real Ulrika Johnson with my four by four! Lynn was amazing as always and again I was scanned and reassured every two weeks. Considering I'd been told at one hospital appointment after Jessie was born that my chances of having a baby with serious life-threatening complications was at least 1 in 4, I was so lucky to be carrying another healthy baby. We decided to find out the sex at the sixteen week scan and it confirmed our suspicions that we were having a boy. Kian was going to be a big brother! We were all thrilled.

Around this time, I left college without finishing my course. I was disappointed but felt it just wasn't the right time. I had also stopped working at the pub a few months before. It seemed pointless me working on a Saturday night and Ryan going out with his friends while I was busy pulling pints. It was good that we had our weekends back to spend together and we often stayed in with Kian watching The X Factor or Britain's Got Talent; content in our little bubble.

Our wedding day arrived. It was fabulous from start to finish. I just managed to squeeze into my dress and my mum said my bump had purposefully stayed in until after the big day. Ryan's best men, Pete and

Steven, managed to forget the rings between them but that was the only hiccup. My two sisters and Ryan's two sisters looked beautiful as bridesmaids and Kian was our little page boy, with Grace the flower girl. Everyone laughed as they tottered down the aisle whist being bribed with Haribo sweets as a reward to walk sensibly. As we set of for our two-night honeymoon to Aldwark Manor Spa hotel, we all noticed that my bump had well and truly popped out! Little did I know that thirteen years later we would still be going back there every year for our anniversary, staying in the same room. We are little romantics. Ryan's Grammy would call us "Dick and Liddy" (this is a local term used in Yorkshire to describe a devoted couple).

When I started to produce milk at twenty-eight weeks, everyone was convinced I would have our baby early. My bump was quite small and I had to go to hospital for growth scan towards the end of the pregnancy. After almost giving birth in the car with Kian, I had told everyone that I would get to the hospital in plenty of time. We rushed to the hospital as soon as I started contracting nicely at five days overdue, but as it happened, this baby didn't make an appearance for another twenty-four hours. He arrived on Yorkshire Day, the 1st August at 7.30pm weighing a whopping 9lb! It was a shock that he was so big as my bump had only been small and he hadn't been so large at the last growth scan. Ryan was the perfect birth partner. He was calm and didn't fuss me. I didn't have any pain relief apart from gas and air, which wasn't really my choice! I seemed to progress from one centimetre dilated to ten centimetres in a very short space of time. Poor Ryan!

When the baby was born Ryan's face was a picture. My little man was born in his waters, so when he came bursting out onto the bed, popping like a giant balloon, everyone in the room gasped. There hadn't been any blood or mucus during the birth and then suddenly everything at once! It is supposed to be good luck when a baby is born in their waters and we certainly felt very lucky! The elation was short lived, though, as he was quickly whipped away and checked over in the neonatal department. My anxiety went into overdrive. They said he looked a funny colour when he was born and his oxygen level was low. After an anxious wait over what seemed like hours, I was reassured that he was perfectly healthy.

Ryan had his heart set on calling our baby 'Liam' or 'Lennon'. He was really into the band Oasis and loves The Beatles and decided that he wanted a suitably 'Indie' name but when we looked at him, neither of those names suited him. I was dubious about the name 'Liam' anyway because I thought Kian and Liam were too similar. Then someone suggested Isaac and we both loved it. He didn't stay Isaac for long, as his name got shortened to Zac or Zaccy almost straight away. At twenty-seven I was married and had two perfect and healthy boys. Was this finally my time to be truly happy?

Chapter 13: Anxiety hits

It's difficult to pinpoint when my anxiety and mental health problems started. I had never really identified myself as an anxious person, so when these feelings began to bubble, it was certainly a shock. Fiona had been through hell with her anxiety and I had seen first-hand how ill she had been. I had been diagnosed with slight depression after having Kian but that was circumstantial due to the unhealthy relationship I was in and knew I needed to get out of. From the age of seventeen, I had been through so much trauma and had felt depressed a lot of the time but I had reason to feel upset during these years due to grief. Now my life was very different. I was married to someone who I was deeply in love with and I had my beautiful babies who were now four and two years old. I was also working in a job that I loved and had always considered to be my dream vocation.

We had planned a lovely summer holiday to Spain in the summer of 2008, staying in a villa with Fiona, Pete and the children. The build up to the holiday had been a little stressful, though. Zac had been quite poorly and as a last-minute idea, I packed some of his beloved train track and trains to take with us. Thank goodness I did because he spent the whole holiday inside playing contently with the trains, only gracing the pool on the second to last day of the holiday and even then, he didn't particularly like it. His lips would turn blue and he wouldn't stay in the water for long. Contrary to this, Kian and Grace were in the pool constantly and even moaned when it was time to get out to have something to eat. Afternoon naps were the best! When the kids begrudgingly went to bed, we ate late lunch and drank San Miguel in the sun. The holiday was more relaxing than I thought it would be and Fiona and I even got time to sit by the pool and read. I always feel relaxed around Fiona, she is a very calming person.

However, everything changed when we arrived back in England and I felt stressed and upset. I wasn't able to put my finger on what specifically made me feel this way but it was like a switch had been flicked as soon as we touched down. I was content, so why should this perfect storm of anxiety strike now, just when I least expected it?

In my position as the Teenage Pregnancy Officer for West Leeds, I held quite a responsibility. I worked full time but was managing well with childcare and with Ryan finishing work early each day, he helped a lot. My job was enjoyable and satisfying and not particularly stressful, I didn't think. I supported teenage mums whilst they were pregnant and still in education. My empathy towards the girls in my care at work sometimes made things difficult for me, though, as there were girls who were pregnant and didn't want their baby, or those whose situations took me back to my memories of a time when I was pregnant as a teenager. This was always going to be a downside of the job, though, and the satisfaction I got from it seemed to outweigh this. I had regular meetings at schools and colleges with the girls in my care and ensured that their childcare arrangements and maternity leave were well organised as well as removing any barriers to them completing their education. (At one point, one of my clients completed her GCSE English exam at home whilst in labour!). Leaving the Youth Service had been a difficult decision but now I had my evenings back and we were more than financially stable. The youth service work had been a great stepping-stone to working in teenage pregnancy and I had gained valuable experience from delivering relationship and sex education sessions, so I had also set up a young parent's group at a local children's centre which attracted young parents to socialise together for peer support. It was very successful and I was praised highly by my supervisor and by the community.

Zac was completely different to how Kian had been as a baby. Kian has always been resilient, healthy and confident. Zac on the other hand, suffers with a few health problems. Nothing major, thank goodness, but he has been under paediatric care on and off since he was a baby. He suffered badly with his chest and was diagnosed with Asthma and a grade 3 Heart Murmur during a stay at hospital when he was two years old. He was always a snotty and poorly baby and at aged two he had to have a procedure to clear his tear ducts under general anaesthetic. Over the years, he's had to have numerous tests and investigations. When his heart murmur was diagnosed, he was sent for an ECG and an Echocardiogram to ensure he didn't have any other heart conditions. As you can imagine, this was a very worrying time for us, especially because Andrew and Jessie both had serious heart conditions. Thankfully, Zac's heart is healthy and normal apart from the murmur but he has also had Grommets and his ears syringed several times for Glue Ear, his nose lining lasered to increase breathing through his nose and less through his mouth, and had he has also had his Adenoids removed to help with congestion. We spent several nights at A&E due to him having recurring Croup which he needed steroids and a nebulizer administering for on more than once occasion. Zac's health issues were of course stressful to deal with at the time but nothing like what I had been through before, so surely, I could cope with this? The problem was that somehow, I had talked myself into believing that I deserved Zac to be unhealthy because I chose not to go through with having Andrew and Jessie.

We had been trying for another baby and I hadn't been on the Pill or used any contraception since Zac was born. I did wonder if this obsession to conceive would ever go away but this was part of my life now and something I had become used to. Every month, I still became upset and worried that my period would start though because every period would be horrendously painful and debilitating and I would leak constantly and pass large blood clots. If my period was late, I'd be heartbroken when I did pregnancy texts only to find out they were negative. Occasionally there would be a faint positive but then I would start bleeding in the days soon after. The whole experience was a rollercoaster each month and the pain was mental as well as physical and the pressure I felt from this was increasing.

Bedtime became unbearable as just putting my head on the pillow and closing my eyes would cause a rush of adrenaline through my body and I would jerk itself back awake. It was like falling from a cliff in a dream and waking up mid-fall. It got so bad that I couldn't sleep at all and began getting flash backs to my pregnancies from when I was younger. I would lie awake, trying to imagine what my baby girl, Jessie looked like. The guilt of my past decisions was haunting me and I didn't feel connected to the babies that I had lost.

Initially, I thought it was something physical that was making me jerk awake. I assumed there was something wrong with my brain and often found myself in my doctor's office, searching for answers. The doctor said they would keep an eye on the situation and I was invited for tests, but she was convinced I was suffering from severe anxiety which was coming out in a physical way. I was quite taken aback by this diagnosis but have since learned that anxiety can manifest itself in many ways and that physical symptoms are very common. It wasn't as if I was having a typical panic attack, though, and wasn't struggling with my breathing or having sweats or feelings of panic, so this had not even been on my radar as being a potential cause. I was exhausted from not sleeping and the irrational thoughts I was suffering. I was off sick from work and that made me feel guilty as well, only compounding the problem.

Ryan was extremely supportive during this time and took time off work to help with the boys and the jobs around the house. I was still functioning to some degree but was feeling worse by the day. The jerking body movements I was experiencing at night were helped with 10mg a night of Temazepam, a drug that is used in the short term to aid sleep problems. It can be quite addictive however, and you eventually need to take more and more as your body builds resistance. It did help me to sleep at night but I felt like a zombie during the day. My eating habits were poor and I was surviving on cups of tea and biscuits. I was backwards and forwards to see my doctor regularly, losing more weight each time. The jerks began to happen during the day now as well and I was severely anxious and full of adrenaline at the same time as feeling drowsy and foggy from the effects of the sleeping tablets. After a while, my doctor prescribed Diazepam as well as the Temazepam to help with what was diagnosed as a 'Myoclonic Jerk', which is an involuntary and brief twitching of muscles. It can be associated with other medical conditions but is primarily a nervous system disorder. Trying to be a good mum to the boys and wife to Ryan felt like a full-time job. It was hell getting through each day and attempting to hold my life together.

My doctor also referred me for CBT (Cognitive Behavioural Therapy) in the hope that I would learn some coping techniques. I would literally try anything to help the way I was feeling at that point. NHS (National Health Servie) CBT delivery is very structured and regimented in its delivery. It is rolled out to thousands of patients each month and takes place in weekly sessions for a set period of time. If you don't build a good relationship with your therapist though, success isn't guaranteed and unfortunately this was a big issue in my case. I found it hard to make a connection with the first therapist I was assigned to. It didn't help that when we first met, he ate a sandwich whilst doing my assessment! I requested a new therapist straight after my first session, using the excuse that a woman may have more empathy for my situation (and hopefully wouldn't eat a smelly tuna sandwich whilst talking to me!). Thankfully, my request was agreed and I had a much better relationship with my new therapist. This new start meant that I was able to complete the sessions, which thankfully helped with the physical symptoms of anxiety I was experiencing.

I had been prescribed various types of medication around this time including Fluoxetine, (an anti-depressant) and Propranolol, (a blood pressure medication that can help with physical symptoms of anxiety) and was still taking Temazepam and Diazepam regularly. In addition to this, I was listening to mindfulness relaxation talks on my phone, which helped me to calm down. I was so happy and settled in my marriage and with my children but at the same time very frustrated as the anxiety was overwhelming me.

There was no one I could speak to who knew what I had been through, apart from my mum, and I didn't like to upset her. I wasn't in touch with Reece or Mark and found them unapproachable. They had both moved on and I wasn't sure if they even spoke with their families anymore about the babies they had lost. It was a long time ago and they might have dealt with the trauma differently. Terri had been seeing a guy who had promised her the world but it turned out that he was actually married and was cheating on his wife, so she had recently moved back to Leeds to be near her mum. I felt very comfortable that she was close, but her life was very different to mine and soon after returning to Leeds, she fell pregnant and moved to a new flat a little further away, so it didn't feel right to burden her with my problems. My lovely friend Fiona was experiencing extreme anxiety at the same time as me and we kind of muddled through it together with empathy for each other's situation. As she hadn't been with me at the time of my miscarriages and stillbirths though, I felt very alone in my thoughts despite having her friendship and support.

When I poured my heart out to my GP, whom I had a built a good relationship with over the last month or so, she listened as I cried to her over the distance I felt from the babies I'd lost and the guilt I lived with every day over losing them. She advised me to try to face my past and to somehow try to connect with the babies I barely acknowledged or spoke about. The grief and trauma were buried deep within me; held beneath like the roots of Jessie and Andrew's memorial trees. I had come so far in trying to improve my mental health, but I knew that there was something deeper that needed to be excavated and brought to the surface, in order for me to heal. The conversation lit a spark within me and I knew then that there was a journey ahead that I needed to travel before I could truly enjoy happiness with the family I had longed for.

………..

The first tentative step on my road to recovery was for me to collate all the information I had at my mum's house about Andrew and Jessie. The hospital memory cards, hand and footprints and condolence cards as well as other memorabilia had been put together in a big brown envelope and put away. I decided to go through it and separate it out into two sections; one for Andrew and one for Jessie. I bought a pink and blue photo frame and a memory album and cut out the footprint of Andrew to put in the front of the blue one and Jessie's in the pink. I unfolded Jessie's still birth certificate and placed it in the album, then went through everything I had with a fine toothed comb. Once I had done this, I knew that the next thing I needed to do was to contact the hospital.

When my babies were born and the polaroid pictures were taken of them, I was told specifically that these would last for around ten years before the images faded. I was thirty-one now and it had been fourteen and eleven years respectively since the photographs were taken. What if the photos had faded? I would ever see what my babies looked like again? I had held Andrew but the memory of his face was a distant memory and I needed something tangible.

I picked up the phone to contact the Clarendon Wing delivery suite, I was shaking with nerves about how I would go about my request. I spoke to lovely midwife who was very understanding of my situation and said that she would get someone to contact me. Someone rang me back soon after and told me that it would take a couple of weeks for my maternity notes to arrive in the department and then they would be in touch to let me know what photographs they could provide. In the meantime, I also contacted the charity I mentioned earlier called ARC (Antenatal Results and Choices). They support parents if they discover during pregnancy that their baby has abnormalities. I had contacted them in the past by phone and they had always listened with a friendly and sympathetic ear. They are based in London and so it's telephone support only but even so, it felt good to talk about my plans to get the photographs of my babies back and my anxiety surrounding this. It was extremely difficult to articulate the emotions and pressures I felt but I was able to share the shame I felt over not seeing or holding Jessie when she was born.

The support worker from ARC was reassuring and empathised with the struggles I was facing to reconnect with the grief and loss of my babies. I'd been able to talk properly about my feelings for the first time in years and feeling brave due to the support I'd received, I ventured up to the top of my mum's garden. Despite visiting my mum and dad's garden and playing with my boys there, this had been something I had avoided for years. I was frightened of what emotions would be evoked when I saw Andrew and Jessie's trees. It was all daunting stuff, but I needed to do this to move forward in my life and these small steps were helping me to gain some control.

Ryan and I now spoke more than ever about my past. We discussed the importance of the photos and the need I felt to see my babies in order to be able to move on from the cycle of anxiety and depression that I was currently frozen in. After a couple of weeks, the hospital got in touch and I was given an appointment to go and meet the specialist bereavement midwife. My dad drove mum and I down to the hospital and dad waited while my mum and I went in. The midwife was very kind and we chatted for a while before she handed me the envelope with the photographs inside. I fell to my knees in a flood of emotion as I tentatively opened the envelope. Jessie's little face was adorable! She had a big bruise on the side of her head from birth trauma but apart from that she looked perfect. Her little features were small, like Mark's. I was completely overwhelmed and so utterly relieved to see her. I then looked at Andrew. He was very badly disfigured and looked so poorly, bless him, but he was still my baby and I loved them both. I experienced a massive release of pent up emotion after seeing them at last. The unknown had been far scarier than the reality.

I showed the photographs to Fiona and then to the GP to whom I had become close. They both cried with me and it made my struggles palpable. Ryan suggested that I should have the photos copied because then I would have them forever if the Polaroid photos were to fade, which they still haven't. We went together to get this done and I placed my photos into my newly organised memory photo albums. All of this was absolutely a step in the right direction to my recovery.

Chapter 14: Fertility treatment

A few months later and my mental health was slowly but surely improving. I had gone back to work but in a different position. I was now supervising contact sessions with parents/siblings and children who were in the care system. Parents would usually have weekly supervision sessions with their children and I would sit in the room and observe the interactions. The job was again quite mentally draining but I accepted it over going back to work in the teenage pregnancy team. I didn't feel I could go back there as this felt to me like I would be taking a big step back to where my mental health problems began. The new job was only part-time hours and apart from the fact that work was an hours' drive away from home, it was going well. The other staff were a friendly bunch and I was feeling much more like myself now. The jerking had completely stopped during the day and night and I was no longer on any medication. The only issue was that I still hadn't managed to fall pregnant and I ached for another baby. The familiar cycle of irregular and painful periods and monthly pregnancy tests continued and the obsession was back with a vengeance. I was buying ovulation kits and pregnancy tests for fun, spending all of my free time at the beginning of my cycle on forums and chat pages looking for tips on conceiving and then by the end of the month, looking for and inventing every symptom of pregnancy. I'd prod my boobs until I made them sore! I bought tests that were supposed to be ultra-sensitive and spent hours squinting for a blue line on the stick. Sex was regimented and strategic every month, then my legs would go straight up in the air for hours afterwards. The disappointment was crushing. I had two perfect boys. What was wrong with me?! It was an itch I just couldn't scratch.

I aired my frustrations in a long chat with my doctor. I explained that my periods were a nightmare and made me practically house bound for at least the first few days and that then I would be exhausted and pale for the next two weeks before it all began again. She referred me to the gynaecology department at the hospital for my period issues and to Seacroft Fertility Clinic for advice and help on conception. I used my persuasive techniques on Ryan and he agreed to have fertility treatment, although I did have a feeling that I might need more than that, this time.

Fiona had just found out that she was pregnant again and a couple of my other friends were also having babies. It was a frustrating time, as after doing every diet and taking every health supplement to try to conceive, it still wasn't happening for us. The consultant we saw at the gynaecology department told us that there wasn't much they could do whilst I was trying for a baby, as most of the medication they could give me for my period issues couldn't be taken during pregnancy. This included the Tranexamic Acid (a blood clotting medication that slows the flow of a menstrual period and helps the body to form clots to stop the leakages) that my GP had prescribed, so I had to come off that, too.

The fertility clinic doctors were amazing from day one, although they had to be, considering the cost! Ryan's eyes almost popped out of his head when they told us the cost of a basic round of Ovulation Induction, an invasive type of fertility treatment which they advised us to try first. Ryan begrudgingly had a sperm test and I had a few random tests including an uncomfortable procedure called a Hysterosalpingogram. For this test, dye is inserted into the fallopian tubes to make sure there are no blockages obstructing egg production and release. All of our tests came back normal and we were advised to go for an initial three rounds of Ovulation Induction. I would need to inject myself every day until a follicle that holds the eggs in the ovary was large enough to release an egg. I would have regular internal scans to monitor this and then when a follicle was large enough to release an egg, I would have to give myself a final injection. Although slightly daunting, the procedure would be a small inconvenience if we were to be blessed with the baby I desired.

Ryan was adamant that he would only be prepared mentally and financially to do three rounds of treatment, with the hope that it would work sooner. We both decided that IVF was out of the question for both of these reasons, plus we felt it would be wrong when we already had two children. When I agreed to this, I was expecting the procedure to work first time! Unfortunately, this was not the case and after three months of my stomach being turned into a pin cushion and copious amounts of strategic sex, there was still upset each month and not only that but a very painful period to follow.

At the same time that we were having this treatment, my youngest sister Gemma fell pregnant with her first baby. Gemma is one of those people who is just lucky in life. She tried for a baby, and then fell on with twins the next month! A girl and boy who were born naturally and at full term. Just perfect. And I wouldn't have wished it any other way for her, but at the time, I could have poked her eyes out! There was worse still to come. My other sister, Susie already had a little girl aged three who was conceived by Ovulation Induction. She had decided to have another baby via the same route as she suffers with very irregular periods, and always has. Her treatment worked first time! I was gutted. She felt bad for me but it was just one of those things. Heartbreakingly, she had to go through a difficult process as they had over stimulated her ovaries and she was pregnant with quads! What are chances? I only wanted one... and she got four! For ethical and safety reasons her pregnancy was reduced down to twins and after her placenta failed at twenty-six weeks, she had an emergency caesarean section, giving birth a few weeks after my sister Gemma. Susie's twins were due at Christmas and she spent thirteen weeks up until that time in the neonatal ward. The children are six years old now and luckily don't have any lasting health problems. They are little fighters and I love them to pieces but at the time, the emotional strain on me was horrendous.

My poor mum didn't know where to turn. Her youngest daughter had given birth for the first time to twins. Her middle daughter had given birth dangerously early and traumatically to twin girls, who were less than 2lb each and so vulnerable health wise, and her eldest daughter had been having fertility treatment that had failed. Going to the hospital to visit my nieces was an extremely harrowing experience. I was ecstatic that they were alive and thriving, but they were the same size as my babies when I lost them and seeing them set me back mentally. If it hadn't been for the support I received from Ryan, I would have completely lost my mind. I had been a practicing Catholic at the time and often asked why God could be so cruel and torture someone so much. Was it a punishment for deciding not to go through with having my babies?

My insomnia was back big time and I can now spot when my mental health isn't great because my sleep always suffers first. I was in a cycle of drinking wine one night to sleep but would then wake up in the early hours worrying and panicking over anything and everything. I'd then cut the drinking and take a Zopiclone tablet the following night. The night after, I would feel so frustrated that I would just have a sleepless night without any 'help' and then went back to the wine the following night. It was a cycle that didn't really alert anyone to me having a problem. I wouldn't drink a massive amount, maybe just short of a bottle and it would only be every couple of nights, but I was definitely relying on alcohol and sleeping tablets to get me through this time. I have always enjoyed a glass of wine or two every couple of nights and then maybe a big night out every couple of weeks but then a hangover would make me think, as it does to many people, 'never again'! I realised I had a problem when I didn't enjoy drinking a glass or two of wine anymore. I was just drinking to make myself sleep. The sleeping tablets were like a safety net and I tried to make ten last a couple of weeks. They aren't something the doctor likes to prescribe regularly because they can become very addictive.

After living like this for at least two months I decided to talk to the doctor about an alternative. I was aware that my dad had struggled with alcohol and my mum believed he drank himself to sleep much of the time. I didn't want my relationship with wine to be same. My doctor talked to me about taking a medication called Mirtazapine. This is an antidepressant but has a sedative effect, so you are advised to take it fifteen minutes before you want to sleep. This is the worst medication I have ever taken. I started on fifteen milligrams and this was more than enough! Within ten minutes of taking a tablet the extreme drowsiness hit me like a ton of bricks and I couldn't have stayed awake if I'd wanted to! I can only describe it as the closest I have ever felt to dying and then coming back to life on waking up in the morning. The side effects were dreadful and I felt very lethargic and suffered with awful brain fog the next day.

The other side effect, which was terrible, was that I got obsessed with food. I like my food, but I have always been slim and haven't got a massive appetite. Food became all I thought about from morning until night. We had moved into my mum's house at the time as although we had bought a house, we were in the process of doing it up and couldn't really live there comfortably. This was stressful enough without all the babies being born and all three rounds of the fertility treatment failing. The boys loved being at my mum and dad's house and had the chance to play football in the garden with my dad. I just sat and ate all of the time. It was the summer holidays, so we were all on holiday from school and work and in six weeks I put on around two stones! When I did some research about this medication, I found it is often prescribed to people suffering with eating disorders to increase hunger! I suppose I could have done with gaining a couple of pounds but that amount was ridiculous and the weight gain was making me depressed. I had to come of these tablets and did so within weeks.

I threw myself into working on the new house and we soon moved in. I was so tired from decorating and other jobs in the house that I had naturally started to sleep longer hours and was able to enjoy a glass of wine again after a day's painting. After years of struggling to fall asleep, I have come to the simple conclusion that I don't actually need that much sleep. Ryan is a postman and often gets up before 6.00am. He sleeps well and is often in bed by 10.00pm. I used to go to bed at the same time and was still wide awake at midnight, getting frustrated and wondering why I couldn't sleep. I started going to bed later, between 11.30pm and midnight and this seemed to work wonders, as I would sleep through and wake naturally at 7.00am. This is the perfect amount of sleep I need to feel refreshed the next day.

Chapter 15: Women's problems

The dark days were not over. I experienced anxiety on and off during my mid-thirties and when I look back, this time in my life was a little bit like "ground hog day". Ryan had admitted defeat. Conversations about us having more fertility treatment and trying for a baby were now over and we had drawn a line under the situation together. Each month, though, I still hoped that I would get pregnant naturally.

My boys were now getting older. Kian was in junior school and Zac was in infants. Life was physically easier and Ryan and I were reaping the benefits of not having young babies at home. We had also done our fair share of helping both of my sisters with their twins, which was exhausting. I just wished I could get the intense desire for another baby to pass and I wondered if it ever would. My mum said something to me one day that still resonates with me now. She's good at that! She said that I would never lose that feeling of wanting a baby because actually it's just a feeling of wanting to replace something and I could never replace the babies I had lost. Was this true? My mum said, "Jen, you could have ten babies and they would grow up and you wouldn't have a baby anymore, but you would still have ten kids to look after and still have that feeling of loss". I often wonder about women who have lost babies and carry-on having more children. Are they having further babies to replace something? Can they ever satisfy their desire? I have known some women who carry on having children until they physically can't have any more. I understand that some women are naturally maternal like me, but would my desire to have babies have continued if I hadn't experienced such trauma and loss?

My mental health was still up and down and I was getting stressed and upset as I was doing a lot of travelling with my job doing contact support for Social Services. I decided to leave there soon after our last round of fertility treatment failed. Getting a part-time job as a cover teacher in a local high school was a step back in terms of my career but it was close to the boys' school and close to home, so this made it a good option. I was still suffering terribly with my periods and so being close to home, I could get back and change my clothes if I needed to. The pain I experienced each month was getting worse. My doctor referred me to the gynaecology department again and they suggested that I try a couple of months on an injection that can help with the pain of Endometriosis, which they also suspected that I was suffering with. With this condition, patches of tissue that line the womb grow on other organs, such as your fallopian tubes or ovaries and this then sheds like menstruation blood. The injection they gave me is called Depo-Provera. It's a long-acting type of Progesterone. However, you can't stay on it for long because of the risk of Osteoporosis. Nevertheless, three to six months of taking this can help alleviate symptoms, so I decided to give it a go.

The consultant also referred me to have a Laparoscopy procedure, to investigate any issues going on within my womb. This is a relatively straight forward keyhole surgery which is performed under general anaesthetic. The womb is assessed for any Endometriosis or other problems that can cause heavy bleeding such as Fibroids. They carried out this procedure on me a couple of weeks later and found that I had a small amount of Endometriosis and one Fibroid, but they felt that this didn't seem to reflect the amount of pain and bleeding I was experiencing. At my next appointment, I was told that unless I was prepared to try a LARC method (this is a long acting reversable contraception method, such as the Coil), then I would just have to carry on as I was. I had heard that having a Laparoscopy can help you to conceive, so I was not prepared to have the Coil fitted or use any contraception at this point. I just couldn't give up yet!

Chapter 16: Running somewhere

At thirty-five years old I had just about given up on having another baby, it was mentally exhausting to go through the same cycle every month and my body felt drained much of the time. I was quite depressed on and off about the finality of this. However, my boys were getting older now and Kian had started at high school, so I think he would have been mortified if I had announced I was pregnant! I was feeling sluggish and down about my health and my periods. I read that exercise could help and so I joined a running club. I ditched the wine and chocolates (well, sometimes!) and started on a health kick.

As a result of my recent appointments, I went to the hospital to have a Hysteroscopy. This is a minor procedure that looks closely at the uterus and is carried out whilst the patient is awake. It's a little like the more invasive Laparoscopy I'd had two years ago under general anaesthetic but the consultant decided to perform this more minor procedure as he didn't think much would have changed in two year and didn't want to put me through this again. Unfortunately, it was still rather traumatic as at the beginning the nurse seemed panicked and ended up abandoning the procedure. As it turned out, she had found that my uterus was lying in a position that made it impossible to carry out the procedure and so made me a new appointment to come back to have it done under general anaesthetic.

I agreed to have the Marina Coil fitted at the same time as having the Hysteroscopy. It was a big decision because now I would not be able to conceive. I desperately needed to try something as the pain and bleeding each month had now become unbearable. I was having birth contraction like pains which lasted for a few minutes while at the same time feeling like there was something stuck inside me. I would then bleed heavily for a couple of minutes and ultimately, pass a big blood clot. Afterwards, I would often feel dizzy and sick. It was affecting my work and my confidence.

The procedure was carried out and the Coil fitted. The report I received after the Hysteroscopy said I should wait to get an appointment to see the specialist. I didn't hold my breath that this would be anytime soon.

. . . .

Running was going well and although I couldn't run every week because of my periods, I built up to running longer distances, though perhaps not the speed I ran at. I ran with my lovely friend Rachel, a seasoned runner, who was very encouraging. We chatted as we ran and

I enjoyed the feeling that each run gave me afterwards. It's true that the endorphins that are released when you exercise can be the best medicine for your mental health. We did a couple of longer runs and Zac sometimes ran with us as well, he was much faster than me though, and left us both for dust.

Rachel and I decided that we would aim to do the Great North Run and attempt to get a charity place each. We applied about six months before the run for the race in September. I kept seeing that Tommy's charity, who support parents and families who lose a baby or experience premature birth, had places available and so that was to be the chosen one. It would be an honour to raise money for such a prestigious charity. My target was to raise £250 towards the cause. I have shared posts about baby loss in the past on Facebook, but as this was my own story, I was quite scared to put it out there. I was honest in my writing and said in my social media post that Tommy's was a charity close to my heart, and why.

Many of my old friends on Facebook knew that I'd had a difficult past with baby loss, but some people didn't really know the full story and they commented with kind responses and stories of loss that they had suffered, themselves. More importantly, people donated and I raised over £700 for the charity. The pressure was now on to complete the race! I worked hard and felt confident that I could complete the half marathon.

One day, as I looked through the list of donations on my Just Giving page, I saw that there was an anonymous donation of £20. I had an inkling that it might be from Reece. To my knowledge Mark has never been on Facebook but I knew that Reece had an account, as we were (and still are) Facebook friends. Reece is married and has a little boy now. He sometimes commented on my posts and we had sent a few light-hearted and friendly private messages back and forth, but I didn't feel comfortable to ask him outright if this was him.

As I was training for the Great North Run, I often felt weak and tired but carried on through it. A local running group from Farsley called The Flyers met on a Thursday to run and I joined them. The social aspect was as enjoyable as the running and often I would chat my way around the runs, meeting new people. A guy I often ran with used to say, "The only run you will regret is the one you don't do". This is so true and this phrase became my mantra leading up to the Great North Run.

My nerves were shot when the big day came and I kept needing a wee on the two-hour trip to Newcastle. We set off early and Rachel, her husband Lee and I agreed that we would run our own race and meet at the end. It was an uncomfortably warm day which made running conditions difficult. My aim was just to get around the route without collapsing. I needed to complete the run to feel that I had achieved my goal and deserved the sponsorship money. We started at 9.30am and as I ran, there was so much support. We passed through the housing estates to be greeted by people who were out partying with cans of beer. Feeling panicked, I worried it had taken me to the afternoon to get to this point. This, I later discovered, is just the way the people are in Newcastle - they start on the beer early! The last mile of the run was beautiful. The scenery down onto South Shields beach is spectacular. I cried and struggled with my emotions towards the end. I was running alone and a guy helped to motivate me across the finish line. I finished in around three hours and was ecstatic. I just wanted to hug someone as I crossed the line but there was no one there to hug!

I later discovered that it was Reece who was the anonymous donor and not only that but he had been a couple of minutes ahead of me running the Great North Run in memory of his dad, who had been an avid runner. I am not sure I would have wanted our first encounter in years to have involved the sweaty, red and crying me. Although it would have been a poignant moment for us both, I am sure.

Several weeks later I went to the doctors for some blood test results (I had been diagnosed as Anaemic a few months previously). The doctor said that he was surprised that I could run to the end of the road, never mind thirteen and half miles, as my iron levels were very low! The iron tablets weren't really helping because I was bleeding so much. I was extremely proud of myself and what I had achieved for myself and for Tommy's.

By Christmas that year, the period pain and blood loss I was experiencing was getting ridiculous. I spent Christmas Day in agony, popping pain killers and washing them down with Prosecco. I ended up in hospital on Christmas day night bleeding profusely and I worried that I had overdosed on pain killers. This was not part of the plan. I felt so bad having to leave the boys and Ryan to go to hospital on Christmas Day. It was the worst! Something needed to be done and I was now very frightened of what that could be.

Chapter 17: Hysterectomy

I was still revelling in my success from the Great North Run. I had been proactive in fundraising and it made me feel good. In the past I had bought charity cards from ARC and Tommy's, but this was a personal achievement and I was proud. Ryan and I were happy as ever and the kids were both thriving at school and home.

Clearly, having the Coil fitted hadn't led to a successful conclusion and I was now bleeding more or less every day. It wasn't as heavy as it had been previously, but the pain and the inconvenience of bleeding all of the time was driving me mad. I had to leave work on several occasions because the upheaval in my body had now started to make me physically sick.

I received another appointment through the post for a gynaecological review at the hospital and was so worried about what would happen. I didn't think I could cope if I was told that I couldn't have another baby. I knew people of my age who were only just starting their families. How could I have my choice taken away forever?

When the appointment date finally came around, I was quite prepared to be fobbed off with another 'solution' to my problems and to be honest didn't expect any major breakthrough that day. Ryan was working, so I made my way to the hospital alone. To my surprise, the consultant I saw was very empathetic. He went through my history of gynaecological procedures and problems from the past couple of years in detail with me. I had been on Tranexamic Acid, then on injections, I'd had a Laparoscopy and a Hysteroscopy, been diagnosed with slight Endometriosis and Fibroids, had the Coil fitted and had been prodded, poked, scanned and operated on. He explained to me that when I'd had the last Hysteroscopy, they had noticed a drop and prolapse of the womb. He also told me that my womb was tilted, which isn't great for being able to conceive. He described my womb as 'bulky'. Bulky with what? I asked myself. He then went on to tell me that my cervix was weak and wouldn't hold the Coil in place, which is why it hasn't alleviated the problems and why I was bleeding so much.

Having exhausted most of the options, he felt that there was no other procedure or drug available that would help me, apart from a Hysterectomy. What made me really sit back and listen, was when he said that if he was speaking to a member of his family, he would suggest a Hysterectomy because I had been through enough, too much for anyone to cope with and it would only progress to get worse.

This was a huge shock! I thought there would be something else that they could do, first.

The consultant asked me if I felt that my family was complete. I said I thought that my body had made that decision for me. At this point, he indicated that my womb didn't look in a healthy enough state to carry another pregnancy and told me that I would be putting myself and any potential baby at risk. He said that nature is clever and that was why I wasn't conceiving. That day is a total blur to me now. I left the appointment having agreed to be put on the waiting list for a Hysterectomy. When I told my mum and Ryan, they were both relieved that I had made the decision to stop the misery I was going through every couple of weeks. I was concerned about how my mental health would suffer and the feelings I would experience after this major operation. It was November and I had been told to expect an appointment for the operation to be carried out after Christmas, but on the 5th of December, I received a call from the hospital to say that an appointment had become available and they could now fit me in for the operation on the 19th of December. Initially, I instinctively I said 'no'. How could I do this just before Christmas? It would be a ruined holiday for the boys with their mum out of action for another year. However, after speaking to my mum and Ryan, I decided that it would be better to have the op before Christmas, as everyone would be on holiday and I would get the help and support I would need to recover.

It was a scary couple of weeks leading up to the operation. I distracted myself by making sure that all of the presents were bought and wrapped and that everything was planned for Christmas. We had booked to have Christmas dinner out with Ryan's family at a local restaurant and I thought that with this being a week after my operation, I might just manage to go. If not, Ryan said he would bring my lunch down from the restaurant to me to have at home.

The operation would be done vaginally and by keyhole surgery and I would keep my ovaries. The advancements in how the procedure is now carried out means that the recovery time has drastically reduced, so I didn't worry too much about the physical recovery. My main concern was my mental health. After having babies on the brain since before I could remember, now at the age of thirty-six, this was the end of the line for my fertility. Would I still feel as womanly? Would I suffer with depression? In the end, I was thankful for the earlier operation as it meant that I didn't have a lot of time to worry.

There I was on 19th of December arriving at Otley hospital for an operation I thought I'd never have.

Chapter 18: Was my womb controlling my brain?

As I'd imagined, the physical recovery from the operation was relatively straight forward and I was at the restaurant on Christmas day in my party dress waiting for my Christmas dinner without issue. The biggest and most shocking news to tell you is that the anxiety and depression I feared I would feel about not being able to have any more children didn't arrive! As the weeks went on, I felt mentally and physically stronger. The only real medical problem I encountered was a small set back six months after surgery. I began having menopausal symptoms which were unexpected because I'd kept my ovaries, but I have since learned that these symptoms sometimes happen as the ovaries can go into temporary shock when the womb is removed. The doctor prescribed HRT patches, as the heart palpitations and hot sweats I began to experience were unbearable. On one occasion, I was kept in hospital overnight for several tests, including ECG's and twenty-four-hour heart monitoring because my heart was racing and my blood pressure was high. On being discharged from the hospital, I was told that the symptoms were due to the drastic hormonal changes in my body. Unfortunately, the HRT caused me to have debilitating migraines that were utterly terrifying. My vision would be strained, and my heart would pound scarily fast and once, the shaking and sweating was so bad, I thought I was actually dying and called an ambulance! It was very frightening, as migraines were new to me and I didn't understand what was happening.

My doctor took me off HRT and prescribed me blood pressure tablets to slow my heart rate and lower my blood pressure. I was also given Citalopram, which is anti-depressant commonly used for women experiencing menopausal symptoms. I still take this medication now and it has become a normal part of my routine. I am not sure when or if I will ever feel ready to come of this medication.

There is often very conflicting information and medical opinion about how your ovaries will function after having a Hysterectomy. I believe it depends very much on the individual and if you have a good understanding of your body you can check yourself for signs that you are ovulating. One doctor, who is based at my doctor's surgery, is very knowledgeable about the menopause and informed me that the blood supply to the ovaries is gradually cut off within five years to the point where they no longer function at all. Some professionals would say that depending on your age at the time of the Hysterectomy, your ovaries could still work until you would naturally have gone into the menopause. I believe that my ovaries never recovered from the shock of having my uterus removed and gave up the go permanently!

Six weeks after the operation, my mum and I went for a follow up appointment at the gynaecology department and I remember hoping at the time that this visit would be the last one ever! The consultant explained that they had studied my womb after the operation. It was extremely bulky and contained a large amount of Adenomyosis. Hang on, what was that? I had never heard of this condition. He explained that it was similar to Endometriosis but grows inside the womb rather than outside organs. It can cause extreme pain and fertility problems and I later found out that it can be caused by carrying a heavy baby. (I won't blame my 9lb Zac for this!)

Following this diagnosis, I joined several support groups on Facebook, where I had access to support and advice groups at any time of the day or night to answer concerns or questions, or just the support of some comforting words from people who understood. I realised that the condition is more common than I'd initially thought and after being involved actively on these Facebook groups for some time, I was invited to take part in a short BBC documentary, which highlighted this debilitating illness. I felt so grateful yet humble meeting some of the women who also shared this illness. One girl I met had been through hell trying to conceive and hadn't managed to have any children due to the condition. It was heart-breaking. Another girl suffered extreme pain every month and has been hospitalised several times. She is now waiting for a Hysterectomy. I was very nervous taking part in the film but it reached out and helped to diagnose thousands of women suffering with this illness who had not heard of it either. The problem with diagnosis is that it is difficult to see the problem within the womb until you remove it, so it can be a bit of a guessing game to work it out solely from the symptoms experienced.

Quite quickly after my operation, a cloud seemed to lift from over me. The prospect of going back to work in a school was not appealing and I began to think about what I wanted from my future. I had always promised myself that I would finish my degree. Was this something I could now achieve?

Zac was due to start high school the following September and suddenly my horizons opened. Now I had prospects and a different outlook on life. The thought of pregnancy never crossed my mind and the maternal pull that had encased me for all of my life was suddenly gone. I had worried so much about feeling useless and redundant without a womb and the subsequent inability to conceive. Astonishingly, this was not at all the reality.

Applying for university was a daunting process. I was thirty-seven and felt ancient to be going back to studying. As I mentioned earlier, my dad went back to university and completed a degree while in his sixties, so this gave me hope. The interview and application process seemed reasonably straightforward and our financial situation meant we could just about afford for me to go with the help of a student loan.

Embracing university and study has been the greatest decision I could have made. It took me some time to get used to new technology and little things like not having to physically hand in your work to the lecturer. My new friends laughed when I asked if I should submit my work to a 'pigeonhole'!

I constantly questioned and contemplated the reasons why my feelings had drastically changed. Medically trained professionals would simply put this down to hormones. However, I would argue it is more complex than that. I undertook a research proposal in my first year about women and how they behave in society and whether there is a link to their biological make up, and to their psychological outlook. I became desperate to know if there were any women who had experienced a similar history to mine. I had experienced a massive biological change in my body, which led to me having a completely different view on life and this left me asking the question: "Was my womb controlling my brain?"

Women have far greater opportunities, options and choices in modern society than ever before. This makes me question the dominance embedded in a female that enables her to make her life choices. Does it derive from social structure and class? We know that some women are born into more privileged environments and that these women might make an informed decision not to have children. They have been educated on sexual health and contraception and they have more opportunities available. However, if women choose to have children young, they are portrayed negatively. They are accused of being uneducated and irresponsible. There are social aspects in society which would indicate higher levels of teenage pregnancy, for example poverty, being in the Care system or learned behaviour. I had options and opportunities but still chose to get pregnant at seventeen. There was something inside me that dragged my life in that direction. Did my brain have a stronger connection to my womb and its' hormones? The Greeks described the womb as such a powerful entity. Could it be really that powerful?

I've since undertaken a huge amount of secondary research which has somewhat varied in relevance. This has involved looking back into

213

history to the Ancient Greeks and their perception of the womb and how it played an incredibly powerful part in society. Female anatomy was celebrated, although also chastised in strange and often unbelievable rituals. Through the ages, the importance of the womb has varied but it was often a symbol of the creation of all possibilities and potential in life.

From my research I have learned that many women feel a strong connection between the brain and the womb. I believe that the physical presence of the womb in a female body with its' hormones, chemicals and adrenal messages has a huge effect on the brain, our daily thoughts and how we as women feel about ourselves and our physical bodies, whether or not we realise it.

While completing my degree, I decided that I wanted to get back into working within the local community. Fiona had started volunteering at a charity called Home-Start alongside her study and was finding it really rewarding. There is a network of over 200 Home-Start communities across the U.K with around 13,000 trained volunteers supporting families with various struggles including post-natal depression, bereavement or just general parental struggles. I decided to complete the training program, which is quite intense and takes place once a week for three hours over a period of a few months. It was a breath of fresh air to do this training alongside my studies and it gave me confidence that I was heading in the right direction for my future. I worked with some wonderful people and after the training, my local Home-Start asked me to support a vulnerable teenage parent with severe complex needs. Working with a teenage parent felt completely different this time compared to when I worked in this area before. I felt so much more confident and able to deal with my own emotions. I have since attended various training sessions with Home-Start Leeds and highly commend the support they give to their volunteers and families. I continue to volunteer with families, but this has been a little difficult in the current climate (as I write, we are in a U.K-wide lockdown due to the Covid-19 pandemic).

Now at work and in my studies, I try to harness my own experiences and enjoy exploring theories and putting them into practice. I completed my dissertation on Teenage pregnancy. This involved looking at government policy changes and how and why the level of teenage pregnancy has dropped in the U.K over the past twenty years. Statistically, a high percentage of teenage parents in the U.K today come from the Care system and have a poor education or are unemployed, so therefore are at a much higher risk of having complex needs including living in poverty and suffering with depression. This is an unfortunate situation for this small and vulnerable group within society, whose lack of education and confidence often stems from childhood and not from their own choices. I have always said that young parents make brilliant parents. They have the energy and enthusiasm to succeed and generally want the best outcomes for their children. I would love to see more government funding to support these parents and advocate for this wherever I can.

I received a 1st for my dissertation and was proud of the work I had produced. It was hard graft, but I am passionate about the theories and policies and this showed in the final culmination of my degree. I now have the qualification to match my varied experience.

....

For me, having my womb removed was like being set free from prison but I could never have dreamed in a million years that this would be the case, and only felt this way after I'd had the operation. I will be eternally grateful for my boys but I have certainly been through a love/hate relationship with the womb they came from, especially over the past few years. Some women may relate to the experiences I have had as a woman, and others not although I expect that many women will resonate with certain emotions including the sadness, happiness, guilt and pain connected to being female. Watching Caroline Flack (God rest her soul) being interviewed by Kathy Burke about being single, she described her guilt over not feeling 'wired up to having children', and at forty years old she had wondered if the time would ever be right. My body and mind have failed me and rewarded me over the years. However, I don't feel I need to carry a womb around like a heavy bag of shopping anymore. I am now free and truly happy without it.

Chapter 19: Living in the present

I had thought that seeing my babies' photographs would bring me the closure that I needed, and it did for a time. I had come so far with my mental health after the Hysterectomy, but the fact that Andrew was born one day short of us being able to register him as a legal birth had always played on my mind. I was able to register Jessie's birth and she will be a legal part of my history, whereas Andrew is not because he was born just one day short of the legal birth limit. I had always thought that I may have been further on in the pregnancy with Andrew than had been documented at his birth and it was niggling at me that I didn't have any proof of this. It was time to try to piece together this part of my past, once and for all.

The last part of the jigsaw was for me to get hold of my full maternity notes from the hospital where I gave birth to Jessie, Andrew, Kian and Isaac. I was concerned that the process of looking back into my history could affect me deeply (and potentially adversely) and I worried about the effect that this could have on my family, but I knew that this was something that I had to do. This would be the final part of my journey back to my lost babies.

Getting access to my notes was a long and laborious process. Emails were sent back and forth and I had a constant underlying worry that the notes may have been destroyed. My interest in medicine is long standing, from when my only reference was the big medical book on the shelf at my mum's house. I had even considered becoming a nurse at one point years ago and would have gone for it, if I hadn't been so squeamish about blood and needles. I often watch medical programs and read up about medication. I felt impatient to get my hands on what could be the final part of the puzzle.

When I eventually received all two hundred pages from PALS (Patient Advice and Liaison Services), I was overwhelmed and didn't dare open the envelope to read them. I had no idea what the envelope contained and was scared that there wouldn't be any information from my pregnancy with Andrew because it had been such a long time since his birth now, over twenty years, and deep down I also still felt that the hospital might be hiding something from me!

The big envelope lay unopened for at least two weeks. My heart beat frantically every time I almost plucked up the courage to open it. Eventually, I decided to take the notes to the female GP who I am close to. I explained my fears as I sat with the envelope held tightly in my arms, desperate to know if there were any of Andrew's notes inside. She calmly opened the envelope. She flicked through the notes and told me that there seemed to be an abundance of notes from 1998! It was a massive relief! I could breathe again!

When I returned home, it was as if I had opened a treasure trove. Once I had started, I couldn't stop reading. Some of the handwritten notes were illegible, (due to being written by doctors, who are of course well known for this!) which was very frustrating. The medical terms used were complicated to understand and Google became my companion in helping me to decipher them. My plan was to organise the notes into records for Jessie and Andrew separately and I began coding the information with pink and blue markers in the corner of each page and then into date order. Using the letters and notes, I began to build timelines for when I was pregnant, each birth and the aftercare for both babies. There weren't any notes for Kian and Zac as I had requested the notes between certain dates. Given the size of the envelope I had received, I guess that my medical file is as bulky as my womb was!

It was hard reading and I felt the strong emotions of what I had experienced initially as a child of seventeen and then as a young adult of twenty-one. At first, I thought I would always want to keep the notes private, but despite the strange feeling that I am imparting intimate details about my life with the world in writing this book, I think it is important to share the medical perspective with you alongside my own memories and feelings as they too help to illustrate my experiences. It was a hard decision for me to make, though I'm sure you will be respectful of the personal information held within these pages.

These notes have also given me the hard evidence that the decisions I made were the correct ones. Despite now having my full medical notes and having poured over them for answers, I am still unsure about the dates that I was pregnant with Andrew and don't think I will ever get closure on this aspect. When I try to work out my dates from the documentation, my pregnancy was a week ahead of what was recorded at the birth, so I was almost twenty-five weeks pregnant and not almost twenty-four. It was only in my labour notes that the consultant in charge wrote that he would date the baby as being 23 weeks and 6 days old. It seems quite convenient that this was one day before I would have to go through registering Andrew's birth. Perhaps he thought that this would be too big a burden to carry for the rest of my life? He might have thought this was a typical teenage pregnancy and could be brushed under the carpet, saving me from more pain at my age? I wasn't a typical teenage parent, though. I had a very supportive network and was planning to continue with my education. I could be completely wrong in my suspicions and my GP confirmed to me that had the consultant done this, it would have been unethical.

I must now ask myself whether this knowledge is that important in my life. I can't change the past and the fact is that Andrew's birth wasn't registered and it's something I can't do anything about. I have since been involved in social media campaigns led by the actress and singer Kim Marsh that aim to grant parents legal recognition of a baby loss if it happens before the 24-week cut-off date. This gap in my history has given me another important reason to keep the memories of both of my angel babies alive. I have a tattoo of Andrew and Jessie's footprints on each of my feet and had a picture made with all four of my babies' names, dates of birth, weight and time they were born, which is displayed in my house. I feel so proud when I look at it.

. . . .

We eventually pulled through this difficult time as a family. Family is everything at the end of the day. Over the years, there have been disagreements and upset between me and my sisters, but since my dad became poorly with his heart and my mum was diagnosed as type one diabetic, we have all made a concerted effort to stay close and support each other. We all live within five minutes of each other and probably don't spend as much quality time together as we should, but we help each other out and our children have close relationships. We often bump into each other or see each other's children at the hub that is mum and dad's house and if there is a family crisis, we all pull together. Recently, my whole family went away for the weekend to celebrate my mum and dad's 40th wedding anniversary, where we reconnected as the strong family unit that we are.

It felt like a massive breakthrough for me when I felt able to talk to my boys about my baby losses. I found my experiences extremely difficult to articulate at first, but I needed to be open and honest with them and they were at an age where they could understand what I had been through to some extent. It was a lot for them to take in. They asked some questions at the time and I hope now that everything is out in the open, they would feel able to talk to me more about Andrew and Jessie, if they ever wanted to. Facing speaking to my boys has also helped me to be able to talk with my friends about my experiences, too.

I remember due dates and birthdays openly now and I released a pink balloon on Jessie's eighteenth birthday. I always remember the song 'Mama' by the Spice Girls which was released just after I lost Jessie. The words of the song are so poignant and remind me of my angel babies. Despite my Catholic upbringing, I am not massively religious. Nevertheless, I like to hope my angels are now in heaven, out of pain and at peace.

. . . .

My mental health has continued to improve over time. I have spent a lot of time over the past few years reading and researching to try to understand more about trauma and what affect it can have on our lives, and this new knowledge has been invaluable to my recovery. Although I have never been officially diagnosed with post-traumatic stress disorder, the psychological symptoms I have lived with for over twenty years certainly fit with the documented symptoms of PTSD. This awful illness does not only affect war veterans and society has now become aware of a variety of traumatic instances that can cause PTSD. For example, a traumatic birth can sometimes lead to a woman being stuck with an imprint of this event in her mind and she is often unable to escape the flashbacks to the pain and horrors of what has occurred. Imagine having to deal with these sensations whilst pregnant again! Visiting the same hospital for appointments, going into the same delivery suite or theatre where the same smells and surroundings take you back to the traumatic event, and whilst everyone around you expects you to be positive about a new pregnancy. Such experiences can cause depression and anxiety to manifest in a woman and for many, the perinatal period can have devasting effects on a woman's journey through pregnancy and birth.

Not being diagnosed whilst I was suffering with flashbacks, nightmares and myoclonic jerks is frustrating. Mental health diagnosis and recognition has advanced massively in recent years and when I describe my symptoms to doctors now, they agree that PTSD is definitely something that describes my symptoms. A book which has become like a bible to me is 'The Body Keeps the Score' by Bessel van der Kolk, which was recommended to me by my friend Laura. (She is now also a fellow literary expert in mental health and is completing a degree herself.) Mr. van der Kolk has been one of the world's foremost experts on traumatic stress for the past 30 years. He runs a trauma centre in Boston, U.S.A but is also a founder professor and psychiatrist at Boston University. In his book, he talks about the memories of trauma and the incidences where you have felt 'alive' in those moments. Even though my experiences were traumatic, I can totally relate to this. I often mentally threw myself back to the traumatic times of being pregnant and became obsessed with wanting to feel how I did previously because it felt more vivid and real than having to deal with the present. This is rather distressing because you miss out on the simple pleasures of what is going on around you and everyday experiences like playing with your children can become daunting because of the brain fog you are experiencing. When I look back now, I had a habit of doing this when I worked for the teenage pregnancy team. I was constantly thinking back to being a pregnant teenager and giving birth. I would get flashbacks and relive my experiences over and over in my head. It was exhausting.

. . . .

Having been through and come out at the other side of the experiences I have endured; I have become a more empathetic and resilient person. Due to this newfound strength, I am now well equipped to help and support others who have experienced baby loss, had a medical reason for a termination, or gynaecological problems. The number of midwives and doctors who didn't take into account that I had been through labour twice before I had Kian was very upsetting for me during labour. Being back in the same hospital to give birth can bring back traumatic memories and the loss and heartache can hit new parents hard, even though they have now had a healthy pregnancy and birth.

I didn't have the best experience in hospital when giving birth to Kian and Zac and my own experiences led me to set up the Rainbow Baby charity. In recent years, I have met with medical teams at LGI to talk to them about the issues that women face in pregnancy and labour and advocated for specific needs around previous baby loss for women in labour to be taken more seriously by professionals when they assess or care for a patient, which has now been taken on board. With the knowledge that a woman has been through previous baby loss, a professional will automatically show empathy, rather than making assumptions and thanks to the insight I've provided to healthcare teams at LGI, some midwives there now even refer to 'termination for medical reasons' as 'compassionate induction'; a much softer phrase than its' predecessor! It is sometimes difficult for women to articulate what and how they feel and what they have experienced, especially when they are in labour(!) and if a professional is aware of their history, it makes the woman's/couples story and past feel valuable and 'real' for them in their experience of birth. If there is some support offered or something extra that would make a new mum feel more comfortable, the woman will feel that she is in an environment where she can talk to someone who can be proactive in making her feel at ease. This is where my charity can help.

Last year, I was asked to speak to over two hundred people about my charity work. I raised money by selling Rainbow Baby branded vests on social media and within my local community. With the money this raised, I then had over two hundred rainbow design vests made to give to parents at the Clarendon Wing who had a new baby after having previously suffered a miscarriage or still birth. (Alongside the vest was written support information on agencies who can help with baby loss). The Rainbow Baby vest and sticker are now given to pregnant women in hospital to indicate to those caring for her that she has had a previous baby loss. Rainbow Baby now also provides care packages to the LGI for women in hospital experiencing or following a loss. These include essential toiletries required for stay in hospital.

Working on this fundraising enterprise is an uplifting experience for me and it is wonderful to be able to support other families after the trauma of a loss. Last year, I organised a service at our local Parish Church on Baby Loss Awareness Day. This was a moving service that touched many families. I support local baby loss charities as much as I can and all of this has helped me hugely on my road to recovery.

I love that families now receive a Rainbow Baby vest if they have had a previous loss and I hope it brings them a better experience of birth and a newfound peace with their rainbow baby. Their new babies are special and it's true that they can be the sunshine at the end of the storm for many families, so it's very satisfying for me to be part of a project that can help new mums and parents to make their experiences more bearable.

My advice to anyone talking to women who they don't know very well, either on a personal or professional level, is to never 'assume'. I know I would never ask a woman who had just got married if she was going to try for a baby. In fact, I never ask anyone about pregnancy or birth unless I know someone's history, or they volunteer information to me. I cringe at baby showers sometimes because of the questions and conversations that are brought up. I have been asked several times if I am going to try for a baby girl. Thankfully, this happens less now that I have had a Hysterectomy. Fertility is another bug bare of mine. Questioning women as to whether they will give their baby a sibling or whether they are going to have another baby. Wow! The pressure that some women are under! Pregnancy is one of the only things in life that that you can't plan. I know several career women who have always got what they wanted, when they wanted in terms of qualifications, jobs etc., but trying to plan a baby can be a whole different ball game that can cause stress and anxiety for many women who struggle to conceive or are unable to conceive when planned.

Now, with the platform that is social media, there is an abundance of support groups that were not available to me when I gave birth to Jessie and Andrew. The kindness and support that strangers offer each other when they are going through or have had a baby loss amazes me. I know there is controversy over social media and there are always individuals who spoil things, but the groups I have been part of have always provided care, support and great comfort for people. I recall feeling so isolated when I gave birth to Andrew and Jessie, like I was the only person in the world who was going through this, so these groups would have been priceless to me at the time. Although it does need to be used wisely: We must tell ourselves that social media is not the real world and it is often unrealistic. My lovely sisters-in-law both have young boys and I have enjoyed being part of their 'baby showers' and 'gender reveal' parties. At first, it was difficult to accept that these are now part of modern pregnancy, especially when my first pregnancies ended so tragically. I do try hard not to pass my anxieties over pregnancy on to others but it still makes me feel anxious to celebrate a baby before its born. I suppose this is not unusual for someone who has been through baby loss. I personally wouldn't even have a pram in my house until each of my boys arrived.

....

My boys are getting older now and both are almost teenagers. Zac has grown out of his chest issues now, though he still suffers regularly with bad coughs. He has always been a sporty boy and plays football and rugby, takes part in athletics and gets involved in just about any other sport he can, just like his grandad. I am sure that all of this exercise helps with keeping his chest issues under control as he deals with illness very well now. They are truly my world and am so grateful and proud to be their mum. We love 'family time', but Kian and Zac have their own friends and interests these days, which means that Ryan and I can now enjoy some time together after fourteen years bringing up children. I have a wonderful relationship with my mum and grandma. We are three generations of strong women. My grandma is ninety years old now. She has had a difficult time recently, having lost her brother and sister but while she has teary moments, she's still putting her make up on every day and doing her hair. She is a glamorous granny and adored by her five children, fifteen grandchildren and over twenty great grandchildren! I've actually lost count, but she never misses a birthday! She is so strong and I admire her bravery to have come through her childhood adversities to where she is now. My mum is my rock and my best friend. I love her so much. As I mentioned, she has type one diabetes but you wouldn't know it. She doesn't complain and lives life to the full. I can never thank her enough for everything she has done for me. I know I have caused her some stress over the years: From the home hair dyes going wrong, to the sometimes-poor relationship choices I have made and to the pregnancy and health issues I have endured, but she has been with me all of the way. My mum was worried I would portray her as an ogre in this book. I could never do that! She has made me the determined woman I am today. My dad is now in a much better place mentally and I love him dearly. I would say we are very similar people; I stare in the face of adversity, but I also know that trauma has a good way of catching up with you.

Having worked with girls from less privileged backgrounds, I appreciate even more the amazing role models who I have been lucky enough to have in my life and who have supported me through the traumas I have suffered.

....

Two skills I have learned over time which I'd like to share with you are, firstly, to try to accept the past and to live in the present; enjoying the here and now. It's not easy but Mindfulness has so far been an excellent way for me to achieve this. Taking time out to really observe what is what is going on around you at that time is grounding and a calming way to alleviate anxiety. Just ten minutes of practice can give you more peace in your life. I also run or go for walks which I find are both excellent ways to relieve anxiety and intrusive thought patterns.

The second, is to accept the guilt of the past. This is still tremendously painful for me at times. If nature had done what it usually does with a developing foetus with serious abnormalities, which is to miscarry, the guilt might have been physiologically easier. The pain and the memory of any lost child never leaves you completely, even if the pregnancy ended very early but at least with a miscarriage, the decision is taken away from you. If only I had come to terms with the fact that no amount of guilt will change the past, earlier.

I'm elated that I have finished writing this book. The process of getting the words down on paper that were already written in my head has been hugely therapeutic. If my mum were to ask me the question now that she asked when I had just given birth to Kian about having everything that I had ever wanted, the answer would be 'Yes'! What I hadn't realised back then, was that I would need to take some very difficult steps back into my past in order to be truly happy.

After many frustrated nights of writing essays and threatening to throw my laptop out of the window, I am now studying for a master's degree in Public Health - Health Promotion at Leeds Beckett University.

I am now eager for the future to begin, as there is no future in the past.

If I didn't have my struggles, I wouldn't have gained my strength....

THE END

About the author

Jen Palfreeman is a public health professional, mother, runner and charity owner who is currently studying a postgraduate degree in Public Health Promotion.

She draws on her own experiences to advocate for pregnant women who have previously suffered miscarriage and still birth to ensure that their experience in hospital during labour is as mentally comfortable as possible.

Whilst writing this book has been a cathartic process, her ultimate hope is that it will help others who are going through, or who have been though similar experiences to find the strength to come out of the other side of trauma.

Printed in Great Britain
by Amazon